1450

The Word and Words
Towards a Theology of Preaching

The Word and Words
Towards a Theology of Preaching

by

Eric C. Rust

Mercer University Press
Macon, Ga. 31207

All books published by Mercer University Press are produced
on acid-free paper which exceeds the minimum standards set by the
National Historical Publications and Records Commission.

Library of Congress Cataloging in Publication Data

Rust, Eric Charles.
   The word and words.

   Includes index.
   1. Preaching. 2. Word of God (Theology)
I. Title
BV4211.2.R87   1982   251   82-8032
ISBN 0-86554-055-1   AACR2

Table of Contents

Dedication

To Helen and Our Family
In Love and Gratitude,
My *Ecclesiola in Ecclesia*

Preface

After teaching Christian Theology, Philosophy of Religion and Old Testament Theology in Britain for six years and in America, at the Southern Baptist Theological Seminary, for the past twenty eight years, I have felt constrained to write upon the intimate relationship of such disciplines to the preacher's task. Three different constraints have converged upon me to focus my attention. The first is the background of preaching which lies behind my life. I began preaching at the age of sixteen in the small Baptist and Methodist churches scattered in the Kentish countryside in England. Encouraged by my father, himself a Baptist lay preacher, I found myself preaching on Sundays, while studying as a young student at the Royal College of Science during the week. In the end, the urge to preach and to make the Gospel intelligible to a science-oriented culture sent me to Oxford University for training and so into the preaching ministry. I am grateful to the English Baptist Churches which for twelve years provided me with pulpits and responsive congregations. Although I then became a professor concerned with training ministers, I have remained a preacher, never really happy if I am not preaching on Sundays as well as lecturing on theology during the week. What I do on Sunday and what I teach during the week belong together.

The second constraint came through my friends in the American Baptist Convention who invited me to give a series of lectures on the theme of this book at the Preaching Convocation in Denver, Colorado, in

1978. These lectures have now achieved final form in this book. I am grateful to the friends whose response to the lectures and helpful criticisms encouraged me to move towards publication.

The third constraint has been the verdict of friends who are teaching homiletics at Southern Baptist Theological Seminary and elsewhere that such a book is needed in their classes and one has not been available. Doctors Earl Guinn, James Cox, and William Tuck have encouraged me in this venture, and, by inviting me to lecture in their classes, they have given me the opportunity to test my material existentially.

Many of the people in our churches are biblically and theologically illiterate, despite the travail with Sunday School classes and religious education. Even our preaching tends at times to be superficial, too often skimming the surface, tickling the emotions of the hearer, and demanding little sustained thinking. To emphasize the obvious and to elaborate the commonplace in as interesting a way as possible has become too sadly a frequent mark of the Sunday morning pulpit. It is a wonder that often exaggerated verbal travail in the pulpit can produce only a mouse. The words fail to produce an effective Word. But then some of our congregations demand little more and offer sparse encouragement to more than entertainment. Again, yet other congregations demand preaching from the Bible but in the light of an interpretation which fits the Word into preestablished molds rather than by the employment of an informed exegesis which seeks to allow the Word to come through the biblical words.

More is necessary if the Church is to survive and flourish. Thank God there are still many churches and many committed preachers who are concerned that the Word should have "free course." The Word of God demands thought as well as feeling. It brings judgment on superficiality. It demands activity fraught with critical thinking as well as motivated by a kindled love of the Lord. This conviction underlies what I have tried to say in these pages. Our people need to love the Lord with their minds as well as with their hearts.

Let me repeat: the words often fail to produce an effective Word of divine disclosure. That may explain the title of this book—*The Word and words*. This writer is only too aware of his inadequacies, but he has striven to make his words into effective and relevant carriers of the divine Word. I am indebted to three congregations in England: at Hay Hill Baptist Church, Bath; Oxford Road Baptist Church, Moseley, Birmingham; and New North Road Baptist Church, Huddersfield for shaping and molding those words. Wartime congregations demanded relevance, and the preacher learned to speak to human needs and social crises. Theological students at Rawdon Baptist Theological College, at Crozer Theological Seminary and, for twenty eight years, at Southern Baptist Theological Seminary, have taught me clarity of thought and challenged obscurantism. It is so easy to hide behind cliches and to take refuge in "mysteries" which can only be so described because one closes one's eyes to the truth. But, most of all, I am indebted to my beloved wife and companion for forty-six years, Helen, and our family. She, our children, their spouses, and the grand-children have challenged, criticized, encouraged, and supported. Meal tables on Sundays have involved dissection of my words as well as digestion of our food. So it is fitting that this book should be dedicated to them, and, behind them, to church people and students who have helped me by responsive listening, prayerful support, and critical appraisal. My friends Earl Guinn, James Cox, Glenn Hinson, Welton Gaddy, and Frank Tupper have been my encouragers, sounding boards, and critics. This book is a better effort because of them.

Eric C. Rust

1

The Preacher's Final Authority
The Centrality of the Christ

Our final authority lies in the divine revelation to which as Christians we lay claim. First of all, we do not appeal to reason nor to man's natural moral consciousness. We begin with a divine disclosure. Furthermore, that divine disclosure has come to us in history. It does not come in the deeps of a universal mystical consciousness and is not bound up with some universally present divine awareness, although the Christian Church should never deny the significance of mysticism nor the reality of a general revelation. It comes rather in certain significant historical events which are pregnant with the divine presence and activity.

Christianity belongs to the group of religions which rest their claims upon historical revelation. This group includes Judaism, Islam, and Zoroastrianism, as well as the different forms of Christianity. Its particular form of religious consciousness is evoked by the teaching of some historical prophetic figure like Mohammad or Zoroaster; or by events of deliverance in history associated with Moses and his prophetic successors and by the later interpretations and teachings associated with the Rabbis of Judaism; or, in the case of Christianity, by the teaching and personal activity of the historical personage, Jesus of Nazareth.

Yet, among these historical religions, Christianity has unique characteristics. Although it stands within the prophetic succession from Moses and accepts the historical revelation recorded in the Hebrew Scriptures, it does not regard Jesus as just another prophet. Although it accepts the teaching of Jesus as authoritative, it does not revere him merely as a good teacher and rabbi. Indeed, as the New Testament indicates, Jesus taught men as one whose authority was vested in himself and not like the scribes (Mk. 1:22). The prophet might call on men to hear the Word of the Lord, and the Rabbi might offer men an interpretation of the Jewish Law for their own situation. But Jesus relied on no Word from beyond Himself nor did he offer contemporary application of the traditions of the past. He spoke with freshness and personal authority, as one whose authority was within his own person. He was the Word of God incarnate, taking concrete, historical form. This is the uniqueness of the Christian religion—it is concerned with the person of Jesus Christ and not just with his teachings. The revelation to which it lays claim is embodied in the historical life and activity of Jesus of Nazareth. It is he who constitutes the revelation of God, so that his historical presence is itself the divine disclosure. He is God acting and personally present in history. He is the historicity of God. As John put it, in the Prologue to his Gospel, the Word has enfleshed itself in a human life, become concrete in one personal presence (John 1:14). It is faith in this Person, and not the mere acceptance of his teaching, which constitutes the heart of the Christian religion. The authority of the Christian faith is the personal authority of him who in himself is the divine disclosure.

Disclosure and Authority

The Christian is making a responsive commitment to a divine disclosure. In saying this we are reminding ourselves of the essential aspects of the Christian religion. The word 'commitment' reminds us that faith is not mere assent, the acceptance of some propositional truth or credal statement. It is a personal response of the whole personality, a commitment to a divine disclosure which is supremely attractive. Furthermore, the disclosure involves the recognition of the divine presence in historical form as personal, loving and redemptive.

The most satisfying model for the understanding of what Christian revelation is about is that of personal interrelationship. A person is known, not by a mere study of his external behavior, but by his personal disclosure through word and deed. For there is a mysterious depth in the personal, a mystery which can only be grasped as the person discloses himself by communication and dialogue, and yet which still remains mystery. In addition, such mystery is penetrated only when the other person seeks, in sympathy and empathy, to penetrate through such a disclosure into the mysterious inner ego of the other. Understanding comes through a commitment and a love which the other's disclosure evokes.

So it is with the Christian religion. God reveals himself as personal in all his infinite mystery. He takes human form and becomes a part of our human history. The life, death and resurrection of Jesus of Nazareth constitute a divine disclosure. What is a part of history and might be chronicled as a historical *happening* becomes a revelatory *event*, an event filled with the presence and activity of God. But there can be no disclosure, even at the level of finite person, without a person to respond. So the divine disclosure in Jesus of Nazareth was constituted by the presence of witnesses who recorded the divine impact upon their lives in his life, death and resurrection. From being another teacher, another victim of Roman tyranny, he became a revelatory event to those who had eyes to see. They discerned in him a transcendent Presence who was moving out in love to touch their lives.

John Wisdom has described the religious man as one who discerns in an empirically observable situation a pattern which is not evident to others. Religion, however, is a response to a coming of the divine. It is not a mere discovery. The discernment is evoked by the divine activity in the revelatory event. Thereby, what to others may be one historical happening among many becomes a cosmic divine disclosure, a significant historical event. Christian faith is the response evoked by the event of Jesus of Nazareth. It is a loving commitment. As such, it involves cognitive content, recognition of the nature of the divine presence, as well as the feeling of attraction and love, the experience of gracious self-giving which issues in the act of commitment. It is thus easy for faith as *fiducia* to move into faith as *assentio*, but the primacy lies with the commitment and its concomitant awareness of the personal disclosure of the divine presence.

Jesus is history as historians deal with history, and yet he transcends history. As Berdyaev was never tired of emphasizing, the starting point of Christianity is neither God nor man, but the God-man. The Christian preacher is bound to history, and yet he points beyond history. God has chosen to come to us in human guise. We are required to live by faith and not by sight, by which is meant that we can see what the historian qua historian sees, or we can penetrate deeper and cry "My Lord and my God." But our authority for such a declaration is the Christ who so discloses Himself to us. We cannot prove it by historical investigation.

This is why George Bernard Shaw, studying the recorded life and teaching of Jesus of Nazareth, could write of him in terms which differ from those of a Paul or a John. In the Preface to his play, *Androcles and the Lion*, he wrote: "I am ready to admit that after contemplating the world and human nature for nearly sixty years, I see no way out of the world's misery but the way which would have been found by Christ's will if he had undertaken the work of a modern practical statesman" (George Bernard Shaw, Preface to *Androcles and the Lion*, in his *Complete Plays and Prefaces*, vol. 5 [New York: Dodd, Mead & Co., 1963], p. 323). He had the feeling "that though we crucified Christ on a stick, he somehow managed to get hold of the right end of it, and that if we were better men we might try his plan." Here is a judgment of significance which penetrates somewhat into the inner meaning of the Christ happening and makes it an event, though not a revelatory event, a disclosure of the divine presence. Shaw's judgment of significance finds its authority in his own reflective processes. It is his own personal authority as a thinking person, a rational being, that is involved.

The authority of the Christian is personal and it is inward, but it has its source beyond his personal being. The source resides in the Christ. P. T. Forsyth once wrote these significant words "The truth of Christianity cannot be proved to the man in the street till he come off the street by owning its power" (*The Cruciality of the Cross* [London: Independent Press, 1948], p. viii). In this sense our authority is grounded in personal experience, but it is no product of subjectivism. It takes its rise in our redemptive and liberating experience of the grace of God in Jesus Christ. The historical Jesus becomes the eternal Christ, setting us free from our selfishness and pride, offering us a pardon which we cannot earn and which we do not deserve, liberating us from sin to become his brethren and sons of his Father. This is the Gospel which we proclaim, and the authority for such a declaration about God lies in the Christ, his life, death and resurrection. Behind every preacher of the Gospel stands the Christ.

The prophets of the Old Testament were "proclaimers", as one etymological understanding of the word *navi* suggests. They were men under an inner compulsion, who believed that they had shared in the divine council and been sent forth from the divine presence. Isaiah understood himself as a divine messenger (Isa. 6). Amos likened the divine pressure upon him to the roar of the lion and the fear it engendered (Amos 2:7, 8). Jeremiah felt the divine constraint to declare God's word and likened it to coals of fire shut up within his heart which he could not hold in (Jer. 20:9). So those who have met the Christ have an inner compulsion to share their experience of God's grace in Him. This is the final authority of the Christian faith and it is the final authority of the preacher who proclaims it.

> Whoso has felt the Spirit of the Highest
> Cannot confound, nor doubt Him, nor deny.
> Yea, with one voice, O world, though thou deniest,
> Stand thou on that side, for on this am I.
> (F. W. H. Myers, *Saint Paul* [London:
> H. R. Allenson, Ltd., no date], p. 34.)

The preacher shares this authority with all Christians, but he must be peculiarly aware of it. If he is not, then he cannot preach. He may lecture or discourse, but then he is just a man talking. He will, of course, use rational argument and make an intelligent presentation. Reason has its place, but always in subservience to faith. Faith must always go in search of understanding, as Augustine and Anselm affirmed. Every preacher should be a theologian, but he is not offering, first of all, a lecture on intellectual truth. He is not calling for an assent to a creed or the acceptance of a theological doctrine. He is declaring the living truth, the Good News about God in Jesus the Christ. He is calling for personal commitment to the self-giving love of God disclosed in the Christ event. He is pleading in Christ's stead that men accept in faith the grace so freely offered. The authority of his message is the authority of the Christ who pleads through him.

Kierkegaard was always careful to affirm this by declaring that "truth is subjectivity." By such a statement he did not mean that truth, the truth about man and human existence, is a subjective product. Rather such truth is encountered from beyond in personal form and demands personal commitment. It is both objective and inward. In one of his writings, the great Danish thinker differentiates between the apostle and the professor of theology. His thought may help to drive home our definition of the nature of preaching. The apostle witnessed to the grace of God in Jesus and was persecuted for so doing. The professor is an observer.

Kierkegaard pictures such a man at the scene of the crucifixion who beholds the catastrophic scene and later sees the cruel persecutions meted out to the apostolic witnesses. But he becomes a professor, studying the apostolic history, but not living apostolically. He studies the drama of the crucifixion but is never crucified with Christ. To quote Kierkegaard: "So it ended with the Apostles being crucified—and the professor became professor of the crucifixion of the Apostles. Finally, the professor departed with a quiet, peaceful death" (see Walter Lowrie, *Kierkegaard*, vol. 2 [New York: Harper Torchbooks, 1962], pp. 507-508). True preaching is apostolic.

The Preacher and the Biblical Testimony

We have already noted that there can be no disclosure without responsive witnesses. It is to those eye-witnessess that we turn for knowledge of the event. The preacher's own witness leans back on theirs. It has been customary for every sermon to begin with a biblical text. Too sadly, such a text has become a convenient peg on which to hang a discourse that has little to do with the Gospel of God's grace in Jesus. Some moral platitude, some pseudo-philosophical material from Reader's Digest, some happy thoughts and sunny optimisms may yet begin with a somewhat irrelevant biblical motto. Instead of preaching to sinners, as a dying man to dying men, we too sadly fall into the trap of giving people what they want. So they leave telling us how much they enjoyed our lovely sermon. Yet the Word of the Lord should be a sharp two-edged sword. It is so much easier to tell people how they can lift themselves to heaven by their own shoe straps than to utter the word of judgment and mercy, of condemnation and grace, of undeserved pardon for sinful men in a sinful world.

The original disclosure is bound up with testimony of the eyewitnesses. And so we preachers begin with the bibilical testimony. Indeed, our own preaching is but an extension of that testimony, made relevant for our day, building a bridge to our culture. The Bible is, in a very real sense, a collection of sermons. The Old Testament centers continually in the divine activity as redemptive judgment and promise. It is a historical record, but it is not scientific history in the modern understanding of history. It is not critical history writing, for it is much more concerned with the divine disclosure and activity in an historical happening. In the historical movement, which ever since the Enlightenment has dominated our approach to man's religious consciousness in general and to the

Biblical religion in particular, we have often been more concerned with the happening than with the event. We have been plagued, especially since the time of Troeltsch, with an historicism which denies transcendence and seeks to reduce any uniqueness, including that associated with events of divine disclosure, to the level of the universal. I would be the last to condemn the methods of historical criticism, but I would remind you that when we do apply them to biblical studies, they should but serve to open the door to a deeper and richer understanding of the divine disclosure to which the biblical records bear testimony. Even the Old Testament histories are not history in the modern sense of historical science. They are histories with a greater and revelatory purpose. They ar econcerned to record God's dealing with His people. They are sermons concerned to evoke a response, to make their readers see God in history.

And of course, the prophets declared themselves to be the messengers from the divine council and to have access to the divine Presence. What are the prophetic oracles but sermons testifying to God's judgment and also His mercy? The prophetic writings are collections of sermons that point up to God and forward in promise to His ultimate act of redemption. Historical criticism may help to clarify their life-situations and separate out their oracles, but finally we still have to hear their word as they point in promise to the Christ. It is of value to know that Isaiah and Deutero-Isaiah were two distinct prophets, separated by a century and a half. It helps us to understand the setting of their message. But finally the divine disclosure in Christ stands in judgment upon the partial disclosures to which they testify and upon the fragmentary promises which they offer.

Indeed, the Old Testament is the Word of God in promise, and as such we Christians listen to it. That does not mean that we use words like inerrancy, for historically it is not inerrant. Furthermore, theologically it is not inerrant; otherwise it would not be history. Indeed the theologies of the prophets vary from figure to figure, each grasping in the divine disclosure some dimension of the divine nature and some aspect of the divine promise. The theology of the Deuteronomic school was not that of the priestly school whose members were diversely responsible for the final editing of the Tetrateuch and the rewriting of the history in the Books of Chronicles. The Old Testament witnesses were inspired to witness to God, but their understanding was limited by their culture, by their social milieu, by their times and by their own weakness. The inerrancy lies in the promise of redemption, in the disclosure of a divine grace which transcended all their lack of historical learning and accuracy. We must not absolutize their culture nor deny their historical blemishes. But we must absolutize the divine promise to which they point.

So we come to the New Testament, and this too is a collection of testimonies. We make a sad mistake if we look to the Gospels for a biography of our Lord. As C. H. Dodd pointed out years ago, the gospels are sermons. Once again the methods of historical investigation have helped us to see their setting in the worship of the Church. We can identify specific forms shaped by Christian preaching. But far more important is the affirmation of all four Gospels that God has fulfilled his promise and the day of redemption has dawned. This too is the burden of the Epistles and runs with developing crescendo through the Acts of the Apostles. The apostles were eyewitnesses. That is their supreme qualification. They had seen, touched and handled the Word of Life. With unanimity they point to Jesus. Their theologies vary; their historical accounts do not always agree; they show a developing understanding of the Christ event. But in one thing they are infallible—they preach Christ and Him crucified and risen as the redemptive act of God, the fulfillment of the divine promise, the hope of glory for man and his world. As P. T. Forsyth has pointed out, the Biblical inspiration "does not guarantee every statement or view, even of an apostle. . . The Bible's inspiration, and its infallibility, are such as pertain to redemption and not theology, to salvation and not mere history" (*Positive Preaching and the Modern Mind* [London: The Independent Press, 1953], p. 9).

The Bible is the Word of God insofar as it points to the Christ, the living and eternal Word of God. To use Brunner's vivid picture, "The Scriptures are the crib in which the Christ is laid." The Bible testifies to the Christ in promise and fulfillment, but he transcends the Scriptures and stands in judgment on them as they point towards him in their testimony, clothed in the frail humanity of their authors. There is a famous altar piece at Isenheim in which Matthias Grünewald has painted the Crucifixion and, beneath it, John the Baptist, pointing to the Crucified with an unduly elongated forefinger. That is the true portrayal of the testimony of Scriptures. They point to the crucified and risen Lord, and he towers above them, for he is bigger than the Bible without whose testimony his divine disclosure would not have come to us.

And so we preachers turn back to the Christ as he comes to us in the biblical testimony. The Bible is authoritative for us, but it is derived authority. It is authoritative for us only as it points to him. The miracle is that, as it points, he comes to meet us through its testimony. The Bible was created by faith, and yet miraculously it creates faith. The Christ towers above its testimony and lights up its words with new and vital meaning. Many of its limited insights stand condemned in the light of God's grace in him. The Book of Esther advocates a crude and fierce Jewish nationalism. As an ethical solution to the Jewish problem and the problem of all minorities in alien cultures, it stands condemned, for it ends with the Jew triumphant and the Gentile on the gallows. The Old Testament men could not find a solution to the problem as they grasped for the full light that was to come. Deutero-Isaiah saw further than Esther. He grasped the truth of a suffering servant. Thereby he pointed in promise to one who, in utter forgiving love, hung on a gallows tree of shame and pleaded for his enemies. Apostolic testimonies stimulate us to deeper understanding of such grace, and move us to extend their testimony into our day. For the Bible is creative of sermons in every age. God's Word comes to us through its words, and we too are sent out to proclaim the Gospel of Grace.

There is another secondary authority, however, and that is the Church. Too often we have forgotten the way in which our Bible came to us. The divine disclosure in the Christ-event produced two interacting streams of historical development—the believing fellowship, the Church, and the recorded testimony, the Scriptures. The two streams are so indissolubly bound together that it is impossible to say which came first—the Church or the Bible. From the very beginning the believers were both bound together in mutual love and commitment and were courageous witnesses to their faith in the God who raised Jesus from the dead. Their preaching and worship focalized their common life and fellowship and were crystallized into writings like the Gospels, and into letters like the Epistles of Paul. Undoubtedly such Gospels were especially treasured in certain locations, and the epistles were increasingly shared with other churches by the churches to which they were originally addressed. But as such writings began to multiply and the original eyewitnesses to the Christ even began to pass from the earthly scene, the church had to decide which writings were most reliable. The chief criterion of authenticity and reliability in the written testimonies were apostolicity, the claim that most of the writers were eyewitnesses. In closing the New Testament canon and adding it to the Old Testament scriptures already canonized by the Jewish Rabbis, the church both declared such scriptures authoritative witnesses and also implied its own authority as the community of believers indwelt by the Spirit of the living and risen Christ.

So alongside the derived authority of the Bible we must set the derived authority of the Church. The claim of the latter to decide on the authenticity and reliability of the witnessing documents was based on its claim to be the body of Christ, the ongoing continuation of his incarnate Presence. The Risen Christ was present through the guidance of his immanent Spirit. Sometimes we forget this claim which faith can still make today. So often we speak as if we had not so much as heard of the Holy Spirit. Probably this is from fear of offending secular men who often could not care less. But, indeed, they might respect us more if we affirmed our faith in a Transcendent Presence who is also immanent and active in our midst.

The Preacher and the Ecclesiastical Traditions

The preacher cannot escape the fact that he speaks for and to the fellowship of believers. they constitute his immediate environment. The Gospel which he proclaims is also their Gospel. The Scriptures which provide the basis of his message are also their textbook. He cannot, of course, be sure that they know its text as well as he does. Indeed, often his listeners will prove to be biblically illiterate. He is, however, to witness both to them and for them, to the grace of God for a sinful world. So he will seek to interpret the biblical text and make it relevant for his day.

It is just at this point of interpretation that the preacher cannot escape the traditions of the believing community. Always Scripture has the priority, but through the centuries there has grown up a body of scriptural interpretation and a series of formulated credos and statements of faith. Early in its history, the Church began to build its traditions, adding new theological insights as it sought to interpret and apply to its own day the testimony of the prophets and apostles. Always it acknowledged the basic authority of the Scriptures as testimony to the original disclosure. The new insights were always referred to a scriptural base. In them the Church sought to move to a deeper understanding of the Gospel as it came through this primary testimony. Periodically, conciliar statements sought to offer a concensus of such understanding.

As the Church began to fragment, the various groups within it established their own, often widely differing, traditions.With the passing of time the original disclosure was distorted in the Church's testimony. Its proclamation was weakened and often vitiated. But, again and again, new voices spoke, as the cogency of the Gospel was discovered afresh. Men turned again to the scriptures and became aware of dimensions of the divine disclosure which the Church had too long ignored. Augustine and Francis of Assisi, John Calvin and Martin Luther, Friedrich Schleiermacher and Karl Barth have called the Church back to its original message and a re-affirmation of its Gospel. Yet always such men listened to what the Church, in its better past moments, had sought to affirm and proclaim.

Today, no preacher who seeks for insights in the biblical text can fail to examine the historical movements by which the Gospel has been carried through the centuries. This he must do because the Holy Spirit is still, and continually has been, at work in the Church through all the vicissitudes of its history.

Such authority as the traditions, conciliar statements, credal formulations, and insights of scholarly men may possess is always secondary to the authority of the apostolic testimony and always subject to the judgment of the living Christ who is present in the Person of his Spirit. The fatal error is to enthrone the traditions into a supreme authority rather than to regard them as providing useful guidelines. In the latter attitude, the preacher feels free to discard or ignore such guidelines if they conflict with his understanding of Scripture and his experience of the Christ to whom the Scriptures testify. When authority is vested in an episcopal or a papal succession, we are forgetting that the only real apostolic succession is to succeed to or stand in the faith and testimony of the apostles, for we certainly cannot share in their quality of eye-witnesses. Such an apostolic succession belongs to the whole community of believers under the guiding and enlightening presence of the Holy Spirit. We Baptists find no authority flowing down an episcopal drain pipe. We believe in the right of every Baptist to interpret the Scriptures as the Spirit leads him. Yet this must be qualified by the condition that he should listen to the concensus of the believing fellowship. And that means that he cannot ignore, in coming to his judgment, the traditions and accumulated wisdom of the Church universal in days gone by.

This growth of tradition and formulated confessions reminds us that down through the centuries the Church has continued the task of the original eyewitnesses. It has sought to testify to the original disclosure, and thus, at least in Protestant churches, preaching has been central. In so doing, the Church has to meet the challenge of historical change. The divine disclosure has to be communicated to changing cultural contexts.

Increasing knowledge of the world, new and influential philosophical views, changing life styles and mores, altered social and political patterns—these constitute one pole of a situation in which the Church stands at the other pole. It is in the tension of such polarity, in the dialogue with its cultural context, that the Church's proclamation has always to be shaped. The Word of the Gospel has to be expressed in forms intelligible to the contemporary situation. Every age demands a hermeneutic that makes the divine disclosure in the Christ intelligible and meaningful. The preacher here will be guided by the accumulated wisdom of the past but he will use his rational understanding in searching the Biblical testimony for insights into the divine disclosure which will meet the need of his day. And, always, he will be aware of the presence of the living Christ in the person of his Spirit. For it is this continuing Presence which gives him authority of utterance.

The Preacher and the Living Christ

Our recurring references to the Holy Spirit remind us that we are not dealing merely with a past historical event in which the divine disclosure has taken place. That event includes the Resurrection. Indeed it was the Resurrection which transformed those first disciples from a despondent group into an enthusiastic band of believers and witnesses. Their sermons in Acts recurrently affirm that God raised up this Jesus who had been crucified. Paul, in the opening verses of the Epistle to the Romans, writes that Jesus was declared to be the Son of God with power by the resurrection from the dead. The Resurrection was as much a part of the preaching as was the Crucifixion. If the Gospels are enlarged sermons, the major part of each is concerned with the passion and resurrection of the Lord. So the event in human history is also an event in eternity. The story of the Ascension is one dimension of this, and the other is the continuing presence of the Christ in the Person of His Spirit. The mystery of the trinitarian nature of God at least safeguards the Christ as transcendent in his risen glory and yet immanent and active in his Holy Spirit. However involved we may become in dogmatic formulae, the apostolic witnesses were quite sure that the risen and ascended Lord was still present in the heart of the believer and in the life of his Church. To be in the Spirit was to be in Christ, and to be indwelt by the Spirit was to be indwelt by the Christ.

This brings us to yet a third dimension of our authority as preachers, namely, the *testimonium intus spiritus sancti,* the internal testimony of the Holy Spirit. Our experience of the Christ affirms the original disclosure as the Spirit testifies with our spirit that this is indeed the Son of God. Just as the original revelation through Jesus Christ was constituted by the presence of the eyewitnesses who experienced the disclosure, so the Church continues because believers still enter into the same experience. Kierkegaard's account of this experience is illuminating: "For in relation to the absolute, there is only one tense: the present. For him who is not contemporary with the absolute, for him it has no existence. And as Christ is the absolute, it is easy to see that with respect to Him there is only one situation: that of contemporaneousness" (*Training in Christianity*, trans. W. Lowrie [Princeton: University Press, 1952], p. 67). So because the Christ-event is an event in the life of God as well as an event in human history, in God's time as well as in our creaturely time, it accompanies all time. The Christ is uniquely our contemporary in a dimension of relationship which transcends all time. He is not just a remembered past but a past which becomes present. It is this confrontation by the original disclosure as a present reality with which the inner testimony of the Spirit is concerned.

Paul Tillich makes a similar and useful contribution to our understanding. He differentiates between an original and a dependent revelation. What was originally revealed to one individual for his group is actually received for all mankind and becomes a dependent revelation as new individuals and groups receive it. The original self-giving of God in Jesus is the permanent point of reference. Yet there is a continuous dependent revelation through the history of the Church, in which successive generations receive spiritually what was given—pardon and grace from God. To quote Tillich: "The divine Spirit, illuminating believers individually and as a group, brings their cognitive reason into revelatory correlation with the event on which Christianity is based" (*Systematic Theology*, [Chicago: University of Chicago Press 1951]. p. 127).

So the believer, and the preacher in particular, have the inner authority of the Holy Spirit. Our personal experience of the Christ arises because the Spirit testifies with our spirit that this Jesus is the Christ, the son of the living God, the divine grace in action. The Spirit brings with his presence an inner conviction, a confirmation of that which comes to the believer through the canonical scriptures and the traditional concensus of the believing church. Here the preacher takes his final stand. Like Jeremiah and the other prophets, he must have the burning conviction that, in the Christ, God's gracious self-giving love is available for all men.

Such a conviction must be born of the Spirit in his own personal experience of the Gospel.

There is a real danger that men may so emphasize the possession of the Spirit that they will ignore the apostolic scriptures whose testimony the Spirit is to illumine. The inner testimony must have its objective counterpart in the Biblical testimony. Then the Spirit is the true *alter ego* of the Christ. Without that objective counterpart, preachers may go into the wilderness. As John Whale once remarked, it is only a step from the inner light to the outer darkness. To quote Theo Preiss: "The interior testimony . . . sends the believer back to the exterior testimony, which alone is normative. It adds nothing to the written revelation" (quoted in Donald G. Miller, *Fire in Thy Mouth* [Grand Rapids: Baker Book House, 1976], p. 60).

Only with this inner conviction of the reality of the Christ event can preaching be effective as an act of God. The prophet believed that God's Word, as it came from his human lips and in his human words, was active and dynamic. It was an extension of God's activity into history, for it was potent with the divine intention, a concrete embodiment of the divine will. It would not return to God empty, for it would accomplish the divine intention. Its very utterance would set in motion the forces which would finally bring about its fulfillment. Jesus of Nazareth was the embodiment of the divine Word, the historicity of the divine activity and intention. In Him God acted with power and great glory to liberate sinful men from the burden of their selfishness and guilt. If the Christ is indeed present when the original disclosure in him is preached, then the preacher's words become an extension of the gracious activity of God in the Christ event. As P. T. Forsyth argues: "The Gospel is an act of God, gathered in a point but thrilling through history, and it calls for an act, and inspires it. Its preaching must therefore be an act, a 'function' of the great act. A true sermon is a real deed. It puts the preacher's personality into an act" (*Positive Preaching and the Modern Mind* [London: Independent Press, 1953], p. 15). The Christ is confronting the hearers through the preacher's words, acting in their souls, making his forgiveness and liberating love effective. His Holy Spirit is moving in men's hearts. The Cross and the Resurrection become living realities as they are preached. Men are crucified with Christ and raised to newness of life as the Gospel becomes dynamic in a preacher's words. Men are judged and redeemed as the living Christ confronts them through the preached testimony of a man to whom the Christ is real.

During my student days in 1934, I went to Oberammergau to see the Passion Play. While there I heard a story about two tourists who had gone behind the scenes to meet the actor who played Christ. They were in his dressing room as he prepared to play his part in the last grim journey to the crucifixion. One of them tried to lift the Cross but failed. It was too heavy! "Why," he asked Anton Lang, "do you make the Cross so heavy?" The actor replied, "I could not play my part unless I felt the weight of the Cross." That is a word for every preacher. Only those for whom the Christ is a real and living Presence can effectively proclaim the Gospel of God's undeserved pardon and amazing grace in Jesus of Nazareth. Every sermon must finish by pointing to Him.

> That one face far from vanish, rather grows,
> And decomposes but to recompose,
> Becomes my universe that feels and knows
>   (Robert Browning)
The glory of God in the face of Jesus!

2

The Preacher's Essential Message

The Historicity of God and the Liberation of Man

The preacher's primary task is to point to the Christ as the disclosure of God's grace. He is concerned to arouse commitment, to evoke faith. His appeal is primarily to the will. He is not concerned merely to teach and inform the mind but rather to move the will to a decision about Jesus of Nazareth. His approach is, in our modern jargon, an existential one, and the knowledge of God which he imparts is existential knowledge. He is concerned that men should know God, not just know about him. This is the biblical sense of "know," as when the prophet Hosea calls for knowledge of God rather than sacrificial offerings (Hosea 6:6). It involves the whole person and is a matter of commitment. It is personal knowledge, or, to use Kierkegaard's phrase, such truth is subjectivity.

The divine disclosure has cognitive content, but the latter is much like the personal knowledge in human love. It is immediate awareness and not the result of some ratiocinative process. Since the Bible is our textbook, this is evident in the prophetic and apostolic writings. The Greek way of reason stands in contrast to this Hebrew way of will and obedience. The Greek might argue to God and thus think of him as an idea which made the world intelligible, a rational deduction at the end of a process of reflective thought, but the Biblical writers did not attempt to prove the divine existence or to deduce the nature of such a deity by ratiocinative processes. God confronted them in history, met them in the midst of life. He came through his creatures, through the prophetic consciousness conjoined to natural or historical events. His disclosure was always a mediated disclosure, and yet it came to men with an immediate awareness. They did not have to argue to God from the behavior of his creatures, from the words and acts of prophets or from the events of their historical life. There was a mediated immediacy in their awareness of God. They knew Him and were moved to obey Him.

This, of course, holds supremely true of Jesus. We echo this thought when we sing "Veiled in flesh the God-head see." The Christ takes flesh, yet through His humanity the deity shines, and men commit themselves in faith recognizing his self-giving love as the self-giving love of God.

The man of faith cannot leave it there. He must seek to understand. The insights of faith and the awareness of God in which the religious consciousness originates have to be reflected on, ordered, and integrated with the rest of man's experience. For, as the Greeks realized more than any other ancient people, man is a reasoning creature. Aristotle could describe him as a rational animal. Augustine and his successors brought the Hebrew and the Greek approaches together because, to use Anselm's significant phrase, faith must go in search of understanding—*Fides quaerens intellectum*. Again, I *believe* in order that I may understand—*credo ut intelligam*. The initial cognitive awareness associated with the faith commitment must go in search of a rational understanding. We might say that personal truth has to move into intellectual or propositional truth. *Fiducia* comes first, but because the awareness of faith seeks for intellectual expression, it can easily slip into *assentio*. The preacher needs to remember this. If he fails to stress the living awareness, his preaching can slip easily into lecturing, informing men's minds rather than confronting them with the divine disclosure in all its personal reality.

Even so, the preacher cannot escape theologizing. His sermons will have a theological dimension, but always the rational understanding and intellectual formulation will be subservient to the presentation of the living Christ to the hearers. The appeal to thought is concerned to clear the road for an appeal to faith and commitment. Making the faith intelligible has an evangelical motif. This is our task in this chapter. We have to ask ourselves what is the content of the divine disclosure as it comes to us through the biblical testimony. But doing so will involve a concern with theological understanding, for the preacher and his hearers are required to love the Lord their God with all their mind as well as with all their heart. Such understanding will endeavor to make the divine disclosure intelligible in the light of the contemporary cultural and social context. Current styles of thought and contemporary views on history, nature, morals and society will be called into service where they help to make the disclosure relevant to the human condition.

The Humanity of Jesus

The mystery at the heart of the Christ-event is that Jesus is, in some paradoxical way, God-man. He is a historical being, a man among men. Yet his life, death and resurrection are, for Christian believers, a saving disclosure of God, effective in their lives. He is a human being who is also a divine act. The Christ is history and yet He transcends history.

The preacher should never belittle the humanity of Jesus, his historicity. He was flesh of our flesh and bone of our bones. He has his place in our human story. He was genuinely historical. He was no phantom, no ethereal demi-god playing a role. He lived by the sweat of his brow. He ate and drank, so much so that they blasphemously described him as a gluttonous man and a winebibber. Yet it was a blessed blasphemy, for it testified to his full humanity. He knew what it was to be tempted, to be loved by his friends and hated by his enemies, to suffer disappointment and heartache, to make decisions with tears and bloody sweat, to be deserted by those he loved and disappointed by those in whom he most trusted. He was a fearless debater, a ruthless judge of conventional religiosity, an inspiring teacher, a leader of men. He was a man of joy, rejoicing in simple things, but he was also a man of sorrows and acquainted with grief. He bore the heartbreak and shame and alienation of his fellows. He suffered their obloquy and scorn. He knew what it was to die, and to die a death that, please God! you and I will never die—a felon's execution between two thieves.

In one of his books, Ivan Jergeyevich Turgenev has described how he once had an enlightening vision of the humanity of Jesus.

> I saw myself, a youth, almost a boy, in a low-pitched wooden church. The slim wax candles gleamed, spots of red, before the old pictures of the saints. There stood

> before me many people, all fair-haired peasant heads.
> From time to time, they began swaying, falling, rising
> again, like the ripe ears of wheat when the wind in
> summer passes over them. All at once a man came up
> from behind and stood beside me. I did not turn towards
> him but I felt that the man was Christ. Emotion, curios-
> ity, awe overmastered me. I made an effort and looked at
> my neighbor. A face like everyone, a face like all men's
> faces. "What sort of Christ is this?" I thought. "Such an
> ordinary, ordinary man. It cannot be." I turned away, but
> I had hardly turned my eyes from this ordinary man
> when I felt again that it was really none other than Christ
> standing beside me. Only then I realized that just such a
> face is the face of Christ—a face like all men's faces.
> (Source unknown.)

Yes, real man! His life has the pattern of our common humanity. He
was born. He lived. He died. He was history. Our eyes have seen, our
hands have touched the historical reality.

Yet there is mystery in this humanity. He was tempted as we are, yet
sinless. He loved, where we hate. He gave, where we steal. He spent
himself, where we conserve ourselves. He was humble, where we are
arrogant, and patient, where we are impatient. He was the "man for
others." His life was shot through with love and concern. He never
thought of himself, but always thought of his fellows.

Again, he was the man for others because he was the man for God.
Always it was the Father's will that dominated his life. His mission was to
carry out the Father's purpose. He prayed as you and I should pray, and he
left us a model prayer. He knew the torture of decision, but always it was
decision in the presence of the Father.

The preacher must never forget this humanity. For here is the
prototype of all humanity. Here is man as man ought to be. Here, in the
midst of our human history, is man truly made in the image of God. His
life is life indeed, authentic existence as Heidegger would term it, life with
vital meaning and existential purpose. This is life as we ought to live it,
life in fellowship with God and in service to others. It is a rebuke to man's
conscience and yet it ever draws man into its orbit.

Most of us are familiar with stories about students who decorated
their rooms with erotic pinups until a friend placed a picture of Jesus on

the walls. The pinups began to disappear under the impact of the portrayal of the perfect humanity. The stories can be given sentimental undertones, and here we preachers are often guilty. Yet the deep truth in such stories is that man's sinful passions and crooked life cannot long exist alongside this perfect humanity. Men will either acknowledge their sin or get rid of the cause of their discomfort. The latter is exactly what they did with Jesus. They drove him out of their world on to a Cross. The world would have none of him. It chose Barabbas instead.

Yet men have not succeeded in shutting Jesus out of their world. Listen to Henrik Ibsen, as skeptical as his disciple, George Bernard Shaw. In his play *Emperor and Galilean*, Ibsen makes Julian the Apostate cry: "Thou canst not comprehend it, thou who hast never been under the power of the God-man. It is more than teaching that he spreads over the earth; it is witchcraft that makes the mind captive. They who have been under Him, I believe, can never get free.

So William Hamilton can declare in one breath that God is dead and in the next affirm in moving terms a loyalty to the historical Jesus of Nazareth that almost implies his living presence. "Jesus may be concealed in the world," he declares, "in the neighbor, in this struggle for justice, in that struggle for beauty, clarity and order. Jesus is in the world as masked, and the work of the Christian is to strip off the masks of the world to find him, and, finding him, to stay with him and do his work." At least he is suggesting that the kind of humanity we find in Jesus is potentially in every person. The urges to express noble values and fine ideals, to establish justice and serve others, point to a human ideal which is incarnated in him.

Thomas Hardy in his great poetic epic, *The Dynasts*, pictures Napoleon as saying

> To shoulder Christ from out the topmost niche
> Of human fame, as once I fondly felt,
> Was not for me.

Nietzsche, the father of modern atheism declared (in *The Antichrist*) that "there was only *one* Christian, he died on the cross." Atheist and idealist, statesman and worker, scholar and illiterate, the high, the mighty, the simple—all have acknowledged Jesus' greatness even though they have not all acknowledged his deity. As Emerson saw, the name of Jesus has been ploughed into the history of the race.

This, at least, we preachers can begin with. We are not asking men to accept some lovely hypothetical fancy, some elaborate metaphysical speculation, some figment of the human imagination. We are pointing to concrete historical reality, to a life that was lived and a death that was died. In a secular society, where men deny the supernatural and reject all that transcends the processes which science can study and control, we direct their gaze toward what is empirically observable and verifiable, insofar as past history can be observed and verified. With this at least secular man cannot cavil.

But, of course, Jesus is more than man. He is not just a strange and haunting figure of the past. His historical humanity accompanies all history. He is no "far-off mystic of the Galilean hills," to use Lord Morley's phrase, but rather he is our living contemporary. We read the Gospel story and find him standing forth and judging us, searing our conscience and challenging us with his self-giving love. In Richard Jeffries' classic story of boyhood, *Bevis*, he tells of a boy reading the Gospel story: "The Crucifixion hurt his feelings very much; the cruel nails; the unfeeling spear; he looked at the picture a long time and then turned the page saying, If God had been there, he would not have let them do it!" But God was there! This is the mystery of Jesus. The historicity of Jesus is the historicity of God. The humanity of Jesus is the humanity of God. The life of Jesus is eternal life, for it is the life of God in man, the life of God wrought into the texture of our human story.

We point to that human story, and suddenly secular man ceases to be secular. The dimension of transcendence opens up. Secular man becomes aware of a transcendent presence. He discerns a pattern of meaning in this historical event which is not evident in its historical surface.

> A man may look on glass
> And thereon stay his eye,
> Or, if he pleaseth, through it pass
> And then the heavens espy.
> (Source unknown.)

It is this transparency in the humanity of our Lord which the preacher is concerned to make evident.

The Historicity of God

In this human life we meet the living God. In affirming this reality we also affirm the reality of God. The continuing presence of the Christ is a reality because his historical life is gathered into, and is a continuing dimension of, the life of God. The mystery of his person is the mystery of the incarnate presence of God in him. God has taken concrete form in our history. He has become embodied in our humanity.

How are we to understand this mystery? The Church has wrestled with it down through the centuries and built certain insights, affirmations and safeguards into conciliar decisions and confessional statements. Such attempts to guide and guard the interpretation of the Scriptural testimony need to be respected, as they have been in every age by the great theologians and interpreters of the apostolic testimony. Yet the preacher needs to remember that the forms of expression are often archaic and that interpretations of individual theologians and ecclesiastical confession alike reflect their contemporary culture and employ philosophical ideas which are no longer meaningful.

No preacher can declare the mystery of the incarnate presence without attempting to make it intelligible. If he does not make it intelligible, then he will not touch many modern men for whom Christianity is an unintelligible and outmoded world-view. He needs to remember, however, that the incarnation is a mystery and not a problem. A mystery has to do with the transcendent, with what is finally insoluble. All we can do is seek for pointers of understanding which take us nearer to the heart of the mystery—though it still remains a mystery. A problem, however, is concerned with the finite and the observable, with this empirical world. It is ingredient to the scientific method. The scientist deals with his data believing that they can be ordered and their problems solved, however long it may take to accomplish such objectives. For this reason, contemporary naturalism denies transcendence and the supernatural. Yet the scientific approach to reality has its mysterious fringes, and most of all in the understanding of the personal. Here transcendence and mystery begin to lift their head, for even the nature of self-transcendence is not amenable to the problem-solving method. It is mystery.

Now, if this be true of our finite personhood, how much more true it is of the God-man, to use Berdyaev's phrase. The Chalcedonian Definition is expressed in terms of an outmoded metaphysic including a static view of human nature and a view of the divine nature which fails to recognize its incomprehensible mystery. Yet, although we may reject the somewhat mechanical association of two static "substances," we need to keep the emphasis on the genuine humanity and the actual and dynamic presence of God in this mysterious human life. At best, all that we can offer are analogies or models that may point to the heart of the mystery.

Perhaps we preachers need more than one model, for none must be taken literally, and some are more poetry than prose.

Let me at once say that Chalcedon should prevent us from so identifying Jesus with God that we forget his humanity and fall into the error of docetism. This happens when we refer to Jesus as God instead of remembering that he is "God-man" or "God in man." The error arises often in our approach to the apostolic testimony, for the New Testament describes Jesus as "Son of God." We often fail to see, and so do our people, that this is a religious title describing the unbroken filial relationship of Jesus with his heavenly Father. We confuse it with the later credal use in which the second Person of the Trinity is described as "God the Son." Here the biblical base is the concept of the Logos or Word of God which is the universal creative and revelatory principle that takes concrete form in the man Christ Jesus. Jesus is not the Logos, he is the Logos incarnate. He is not God, he is the human embodiment of God's Presence. He is "God the Son" incarnated in our humanity, the Word become flesh. He is "Son of God" in the religious sense because his humanity was so utterly surrendered to and in communion with the Father that his historical being was permeated by God's presence. Paul Tillich has suggested that his humanity was so utterly surrendered to God that he "is completely transparent to the mystery he reveals" (*Systematic Theology*, 1:148).

We often go to Virginia for a vacation, especially in the Tidewater area. When we go fishing in Chesapeake Bay, we find the same fish as in the Atlantic Ocean, off Virginia Beach. Again, there are just the same chemical constituents in the water, except for the pollution that comes down from Washington! What is the difference? The water of the vast free expanse of the ocean has been poured into the limiting contours of the Bay. We can think of Jesus along the lines of this analogy. The infinite depths of the personal God have poured themselves into the confining contours of this human personal life, so that the humanity of Jesus is permeated with the divine presence.

Another analogy that is sometimes employed is that of a rod of iron in a blacksmith's fire. When heated to red heat, the rod becomes permeated with the fire so that iron and fire form an inseparable unity. The quality of the iron and the quality of the fire maintain their distinctness, but the former becomes a medium for the disclosure of the latter.

Both these analogies are valuable, but neither is sufficiently personal. Since our Lord himself employed personal analogies for God and the apostolic witness points in the same direction, we may seek in this area for some clarification of the mystery of the Christ-event, especially because our hearers today are much more personally oriented.

In the past century much attention has been paid to Phil. 2:6-11. Here Paul postulates the pre-existence of the eternal Son, or the Christ, as sharing in the divine glory and being on an equality with God. Yet Christ emptied himself of his divine glory and took the form of a servant, suffering in obedience even to the death of Calvary. As the sequel, he returned to his surrendered glory with the laurels of victory. A part of an early hymn, this is deeply moving religious poetry and a real insight into the divine cost of the Incarnation. The Incarnation is a supreme manifestation of the divine self-giving. Charles Wesley expressed it in a hymn in which he sang of Him who "left His Father's throne above" and "emptied Himself of all but Love, and bled for Adam's helpless race." The Cross on Calvary reflects the sacrifice in the heart of God. Here is a deep truth and a profound expression of the disclosure in the Christ-event. We can use the picture to drive home the truth of God's amazing grace in Jesus. But when we press the poetry into a metaphysical structure and enthrone "Kenosis" in a theological model, we meet difficulties.

The Kenotic theologians from Thomasius to Bishop Gore and H. R. Mackintosh have shown how difficult the model is. Their general view has been that the eternal Son stripped Himself of those divine attributes such as omnipotence and omniscience by which He relates Himself to His world, and through such self-emptying took the form of a servant. In so doing, he retained His essential Being as holy love and freedom, but he assumed the human qualities of mind by which we men in our finitude are related to our world. This model savors more of the metamorphosis common to pagan mythology than of the Christian understanding of Incarnation. The eternal Son who was God turned Himself into a man.

P. T. Forsyth made a much more valiant and insightful attempt to employ the idea of "Kenosis." He took over from the German theologian, Kähler, the idea of two movements in the Incarnation — one of self-emptying or Kenosis and one of self-fulfilment or Plerosis. In the place of two natures, he saw two personal movements—a subjective renunciation by the Eternal Son in which he set aside the style of God, and an objective achievement whereby he grew toward "the perfecting at once of his soul and our salvation in the cross, resurrection and glory" (P. T. Forsyth, *The Person and Place of Jesus Christ* [London: Independent Press, 1946], pp. 329-30). Thereby Forsyth made a place for human growth.

He still had difficulty, for he had to deal with the sinlessness of Jesus and yet maintain the reality of temptation. Since the divine essence is still present as holy love and freedom, Jesus could not sin. But in renouncing his divine omniscience for the limitations of finite human consciousness, he did not know it, and so his temptations were real. This hardly suggests a genuine humanity. There is, however, an insightful and helpful passage about the real growth in the humanity of the God-man: "... the history of Christ's growth is ... a history of moral reintegration, the history of his recovery, by gradual moral conquest, of the mode of being from which, by a tremendous moral act, he came" (Ibid., p. 308). Forsyth suggests, however, as do all Kenotic theories, that the humanity was a necessary but temporary interlude. The movement of Plerosis means that the Son returns to his pre-existent glory. Once the form of the servant has accomplished its task, the process of the involution of the two movements is complete. There is no clear suggestion that it is the God-man who ascends to the "heavenly session."

We preachers need to remember, even though it is couched in outmoded language, the Church's conviction concerning the significance of the Ascension of our Lord. In the biblical testimony to this event, as well as in the insights of Paul and the Epistle to the Hebrews, there is a clear conviction that the humanity was eternally wedded to the life of the Son of God. He was raised in bodily form, which means presumably that his earthly life and assumed finitude remained in glorified form as a part of his eternal being. He was raised and he ascended as God-man. He accompanies all history as God-man, so that, in the depth of the divine mystery, we have one who understands our sinfulness and creatureliness and who still bears our agony and shares our judgment. Furthermore, he is still extending that divine humanity in the new humanity which is the Church. Christian believers are extensions of the incarnation in time, indwelt by the Christ and incorporated in his divine humanity. Finally, he stands at the end of history, gathering all things into himself, things on earth and things in heaven. He will complete the Incarnation when he incarnates himself in the whole process, as he is now incarnating himself in his body, the Church. And that makes for meaningful preaching!

The personal model still remains the most satisfying, even though we cannot go all the way with the Kenotic theologians. Alongside the Philippians hymn we have the prologue to John's Gospel with its picture of the preexistent Word who tabernacles in our midst in Jesus. Quite early in the history of the Church the apologists seized on the Logos idea because it built a bridge to the Greek world. Today it still has potential significance for us and provides a model for the Incarnation in which some of the insights of the Kenotic model can be incorporated.

Donald Baillie has suggested that our experience of divine grace involves a paradox which may give us a clue to the understanding of the Christ-event. In that experience we can say, "Not I but the grace of God in me," and "I live yet not I, but Christ lives in me." There are moments in our personal communion with God when we know that all is of God's grace, even though the decisions are ours. We remain responsible beings, and yet the initiation and glory belong to God. As Baillie expresses it: "We are . . . responsible persons, and never more truly and fully personal in our actions than in those moments when we are most dependent on God and He lives and acts in us" (*God was in Christ* [London: Faber and Faber Ltd., 1948], p. 117). Our human achievements are ascribed to him, as he takes our broken lives up into personal communion with himself, and yet we are more truly personal, more deeply aware of our own responsibility. We work out our own salvation, and yet it is God who works in us. In being bound to him, we are truly free, truly in his image.

Such an experience is possible because of the Incarnation. It is the Christ-event through which the experience of divine grace can come to us. Then it may well be that this paradox of divine grace is a pale reflection of that paradox that confronts us in the historicity of God, the wedding of a genuine humanity to the eternal God in indissoluble unity. How can the humanity of Jesus be genuine, responsible and personal, and yet he be *God*-man? We are most truly free when we are bound to God, in whose will is our freedom. How much more is that true of the Christ! Though the experience of being bound to God can come to us at times, one aspect of Jesus' uniqueness is that of him it was always true. In his perfect life the paradox was complete and perfect. Baillie contends that this is the mystery of the Incarnation. He quotes Augustine as writing: "Every man, from the commencement of his faith, becomes a Christian by the same grace by which *that* Man from His formation became Christ" (Baillie, *God Was in Christ,* p. 118, quoting Augustine, *De Praedest. Sanct.* i.xv).

So we come to the inner union of the God-man, and seek to understand it in terms of our poor broken experience of God's gracious operation in our lives. This kind of understanding is bound up with the biblical emphasis on the Word or Logos. Since the human word was regarded as a concrete embodiment of the speaker's intention (see chapter one), the divine Word was a concrete projection of the divine being, a going forth of God in creative and revelatory activity. So God speaks in Gen. 1 and the chaos becomes cosmos. So, too, he speaks through the prophets, who can regard themselves as projections, for the time being, of the divine being, media whereby God was especially active in history through his uttered Word. One might almost say that the Old Testament prophets were temporary promises of that perfect and permanent indwelling of God's Word in man which occurred in the Christ-event. In one sense, they manifested in transient form the pattern of God's final manifestation of his presence.

The Word is the projection of the personal presence of God into his world in creation and revelation. As such he takes one human life into his life, indwelling it permanently as, in a temporary way, he indwelt the prophets. The human life becomes a continuing medium of the divine disclosure, open fully to the eternal Word because the humanity is perfectly surrendered to and united with the divine presence. We may speak of a prevenient grace which perfectly surrounded this human life, just as we are sometimes aware that it precedes our own activity. The humanity was, from conception, surrounded by a divine as well as a human environment, and drawn into a union with the divine which was both a human accomplishment and a divine gift.

Forsyth and Kähler, each in his own way, speak of a two-fold movement in the God-man. So we too may see a generative movement of the divine Word towards perfect personal union with the human life. And, at the same time, we may see an upward movement of the human will, a growth of the humanity from surrender to the divine will to a point of perfect personal union with the divine. So the Son learned obedience through the things that he suffered, and found his true freedom in doing the Father's will. Thereby the humanity became a transparent medium for the divine disclosure and a perfect instrument for the divine activity. In such an understanding, we may safeguard a true humanity and hold a place for human decision. At the same time, the generative movement of the divine Word or the eternal Son in gracious self-giving points to the presence of Kenosis, while retaining a genuine humanity.

The preacher declares this historicity because it centers in a divine disclosure. It is this, the heart of the Gospel, which he proclaims. We have seen that the deep truth in the Kenotic model is the sacrificial dimension in the divine life, the self-giving of God in becoming man. When the divine Word, the Eternal Son, united himself with our broken humanity, there was a self-emptying, the acceptance of the limitation of a human instrument, however perfected, and finally the acceptance of a Cross in which the opposition of a sinful world achieved its comsummate expression. The Kenotic self-giving finally lifted Calvary into the heart of God, but then the Cross was already there!

> With this ambiguous earth
> His dealings have been told us. These abide:
> The signal to a maid, the human birth,
> The lesson and the young man crucified.
> (Alice Meynell, "Christ and the Universe")

The Spirits in Prison

If the humanity of Christ discloses the true nature of man, man in God's image, man as he ought to be, it also discloses man as he is. The Cross marks the culminating exposure of the depths of human sinfulness.

The idea of sin does not strike a bell with secular man, for it savors of the gobbledygook he hears over the radio about "sins." The list of sins that some of us preachers elaborate is so long that you wonder what people *can* do. If we could emphasize "sin" as our Lord did, as an attitude of mind which builds life around anything or anyone except the living God, we should be striking home to that widespread sense of alienation and search for meaning which characterizes so many people today. They may not grasp the meaning of sin, but they do feel alienated from the true meaning of life. They are searching for the real "I". As the pop songs have echoed it: "I want to be me". Secular man does not talk about God, but, in his secular way, he is talking about what both we preachers and the divine disclosure call "sin." Secular man is in the lonely crowd, alienated from his true self and alienated from his fellows because he is alienated from God.

Immediately we turn to the bibilical testimony and the fall myth of Gensis 3. Paul can describe the Christ as the last or second Adam, the embodiment of true humanity, because the first Adam (mankind as it emerged within the creative process) had failed (1 Corinthians 15:45; Romans 5:16). The fall story is the story of every man's life, for we are all in that corporate solidarity of humanity which Adam represents. Indeed, Adam in the Hebrew means "man." It must be understood as "humanity," not as a proper name. We all carry in our hearts the memory of the Garden, the memory of how God intended us to be. Yet continuously through history man has refused to cooperate with God. He has taken the control of his own life and of his world into his own hands and turned his back upon his Creator. The root of sin is where it is in the story of Adam, in man's creaturely pride and arrogance, his "God-almightiness," to use Reinhold Niebuhr's description. This is mingled always with a feeling of creaturely insecurity, the feeling that he must make himself secure against both his fellow human beings who may threaten him and against a seemingly hostile environment. He cannot be sure of an invisible reality like God, but he can be sure of himself. He builds his life around himself, or his family, or his possessions.

In becoming estranged from God, man also becomes estranged from his fellows and estranged from the nature out of which he has creatively emerged. The Babel story carries the fall story a stage further. It, too, is the story of all men. It portrays the truth of historical man. Ignoring God, man builds his structures by his own efforts, believing that he can master all things and cast God from his throne in the heavens. But, built upon man's pride and selfishness, the whole social structure falls apart when men ignore God and exploit their fellows. Society divides asunder. Could there be any better symbolic description of this than the failure to communicate, to speak a common tongue! So man, in his sin, finds himself in a divided world.

In his alienation man adopts an impersonal "It" attitude to other persons and his natural environment: "others" are there to be exploited. This is the tragic fact which lies behind the social, racial, political, and economic tensions of human history; behind our technological exploitation of nature and our ecological crises; behind our broken personal realtionships; and behind our meaningless, frustrated lives. Man is alienated and his existence is unauthentic.

Paul Tillich describes authentic man as "theonomous," related to God in freely surrendered self-hood, man in God's image. Only Christ, as Nietzsche saw, is such a man in the perfection of his humanity. Those to whom you and I preach, ourselves included, are either autonomous man or heteronomous man, to use Tillich's significant terminology. We are either living for ourselves or we are finding meaning by losing ourselves in the crowd. Either we arrogantly rely upon our own self-sufficiency or we merge our personality into the mass and are activated by the same sensual hungers and low objectives as the majority of our fellows. This is why the Church has classified sins as sensual sins and spiritual sins. Our spiritual sins are attempts to find security in our own sufficiency. Our sensual sins are selfish attempts to find security and happiness in the passing moment.

Our Lord made it clear that the most case-hardened sinner was the autonomous Pharisee, not the heteronomous publican. You will recall his parable of the Pharisee and the Publican. John Baillie used to tell of a Sunday School teacher who was dealing with this parable. The teacher told the story with emphasis on how sinful the Pharisee was to exalt himself in his pride and to thank God that he was not like the poor publican. Then the bell sounded to end the class, and the teacher said: "Now, children, let us pray and let us thank God that we are not like that Pharisee." Pride can enter the citadel of the most religious soul.

Our sin, whatever form it takes, sets in process a movement of judgment. This is a moral universe, as our Lord made quite clear in his teachings. We have been created with the mysterious gift of freedom. Only so can we truly be God's sons, free to choose, and not automatons. Yet when we mishandle our freedom, we find certain moral barriers in the structure of our world on which, if we ignore them, we destroy ourselves. As Hartshorne puts it, God has set "an optimum of conditions for the freedom of all beings, so there is a balance between undue risk and overmuch security, both of which would be too costly for freedom" (C. Hartshorne, *The Divine Relativity* [New Haven: Yale University Press, 1964], p. 136).

Thereby, sin is self-destructive. Ultimately it makes life meaningless and brings us into a prison from which we can find no escape. The Fall story sees sinful man in the wilderness, the place of meaningless waste. T. S. Elliot's famous poem "The Waste Land" pictures it for us. At the beginning of the peom, he quotes the sibyl, "What is your desire?," and the answer comes: "I desire to die." So the poet looks on the mass of humanity.

> Unreal city,
> Under the brown fog of a winter dawn,
> A crowd flowed over London Bridge, so many,
> I had not thought death had undone so many.
> Sighs, short and infrequent, were exhaled,
> And each man fixed his eyes before his feet.

It is a picture of a culture that has lost its roots and produced "hollow men." So in Eliot's poem, "The Hollow Men," we hear the same refrain:

> This is the dead land

> This is cactus land
> Here the stone images
> Are raised, here they receive
> The supplication of a dead man's hand
> Under the twinkle of a falling star.

And so we read

> *This is the way the world ends,*
> *Not with a bang but a whimper.*

(T. S. Eliot, *Collected Poems and Plays, 1909-1950* [New York: Harcourt, Brace and Company, 1959], pp. 37, 39, 57, 59).

Indeed, T. S. Eliot paints the world in the colors of Dante's *Inferno*. We may not find the world so grim and rootless and hollow. Yet many do. We see this in the literature and plays of the absurd—Beckett and Inesco, and in much of contemporary existentialism with its atheistic presupposition—Sartre and Camus. The absurdists deny the existence of God on the ground that even a God could not make sense of a world so radically absurd. The atheistic existentialists do not believe in God, even though they manifest a lurking sense that such a being might make sense of their world. But since he is not existent, they do not expect the world to make sense. One group begins with absurdity and the other with atheism, but both leave us with a rootless world, suspended over an abyss of nothingness.

The people to whom we preach meet this atmosphere all through the week—suicides, nervous breakdowns, divorces, parent-youth tensions. The restlessness, boredom, meaninglessness of our world penetrate everywhere. People try to escape the tensions by building their lives around position, possessions, status, self-aggrandisement. Our is a "having" generation not a "being" one. Again, people try to lose themselves in the anonymous crowd by drowning themselves in alcohol and narcotics or by taking the road of sensuality.

They may even try the road of vigorous self-reform and moral rectitude. But the morality of secular man is self-centered and sooner or later fails of dynamic. When a man banishes God from his consciousness and does not recognize his actual dependence upon him, he is still estranged however moral he may be. The man who never violates the accepted conventions can still be a sinner. Years ago William Temple once vividly portrayed this—a man keeps the moral rules, then gets proud of his moral achievement, then repents of being proud, then gets proud of having repented, and then begins all over again. We cannot lift ourselves to heaven by our own shoe straps. That is our judgment. We are spirits in prison who need to be set free.

Today many minority groups are seeking to express their Christian faith in the form of a theology of liberation. There is nothing new about that, for Christianity has always proclaimed a Gospel of Redemption. The Good News of the Gospel is that God has acted in Jesus to deliver men from their sin. The disclosure of God in the Christ-event is of a God who redeems men, sets them free from the prison house of sin and guilt. The purpose of the historicity of God is to deliver men. His last word to sinful men is not judgment but redemption; it is a word of grace. So, in the midst of history and at the heart of the Incarnation there is set a Cross.

The Liberating Cross

The disclosure of the love of God in the Christ-event brings us face to face with the place of judgment in God's purpose. To speak of God's wrath savors so often of an outmoded understanding of God as a kind of eastern potentate who will punish any infringement of his majesty. So often we preachers have sublimated our own sadistic tendencies and those of our congregation in a picture of judgment which strikes fear rather than evokes loves. Surely the deeper understanding of guilt is the realization of what our rejection of holy love means to God. God is no angry tyrant in the heavens who rains down his thunderbolts upon a rebellious creation. Rather, when the Bible speaks of God's judgment, it is always in relation to his mercy. Paul's emphasis helps us to see wrath as the underside of God's love, the discipline that may bring men to repentance. The apostle speaks of God giving men over to the sin of their hearts. John Macquarrie can describe God as "He who lets be." In a very real sense this is the deep truth about the Incarnation and the cross. God creates man with freedom to choose, and he respects this power to decide. If we choose ourselves or the things of this world, he permits us to go our way and allows us to destroy ourselves. He will not interfere with our misuse of our freedom except by setting certain moral limits to the chaos which we create and to the outreach of our rebellious decision.

Kierkegaard saw a century ago that this is no infringement of God's power but a demonstration of it. God's power lies in his hiddenness, his patience, his suffering restraint. Kierkegaard held that the distinctive quality of the divine omnipotence is the capacity for withdrawal, leaving the creature free with a degree of independence. So he wrote: "All finite power makes dependent, only omnipotence can make independent, can bring forth from nothing that which has continuance in itself by reason of the fact that omnipotence is withdrawn" (from Kierkegaard's Journals, translated in a footnote in Kierkegaard's *Christian Discourses*, trans. W. Lowrie [London: Oxford University Press, 1939], p. 187). God's almightiness is not the power of irresistible compulsion, but the power of persuasive, constraining, patient love. This is the disclosure of God which is brought to a focus on Calvary. As Bonhoeffer saw with deep insight, when men come of age they tend to crowd God out of his world on to a Cross (D. Bonhoeffer, *Letters and Papers from Prison*, ed. Eberhard Bethge [New York: The Macmillan Co., 1967], p. 196). But men have always done that! As, across the story of time, God has given men over to the sin of their hearts, men's very arrogance and alienation have planted a cross in the divine heart. God suffers in our misuse of freedom, but he will not rob us of our freedom.

Indeed, the greatest mystery of our existence is this gift of freedom. Even God's hiddenness is best understood in the light of this. He hides himself so that he will not rob us of our free decision by overwhelming us with his manifest presence. He comes to us always through his creatures and supremely in Jesus, in the guise of a servant. Even in his disclosure he still hides himself. So Moses found that the manifest glory, the fiery splendor of the mountain top, was veiled by the cloud. We have to walk by faith and not by sight, for there is a kenosis in God's coming. He wills to accomodate his coming to the abilities and limitations of his creatures and to respect their freedom.

In a Paris art collection, there is a painting by Zwingler, entitled "The First Night Outside Paradise." It portrays the man and the woman out side the Garden and behind them the barred gate and the angel with the flaming sword. But their eyes are not fixed on the latter. They are looking upward, and there in the top right hand corner, the artist has painted faintly a cross. When sin entered human history, there was a cross in the heavens. The cross on Calvary brings God's suffernig to a focus in a supreme redemptive act. But what he does in and through his incarnate presence on the Cross opens a window into his heart. It is like the sudden eruption of a volcano, when the red hot flood of lava discloses the fires that have been burning at the mountain's heart from creation. What God shows himself to be on Calvary, he has always been. The Cross is a disclosure of that selfgiving love which suffers in man's rebellion and yet patiently pursues him down the years until at last man turns. This kind of God is indeed the "Hound of Heaven" portrayed in Francis Thomson's poem:

> I fled Him, down the nights and down the days;
> I fled Him, down the arches of the years;
> I fled Him, down the labyrinthine ways
> Of my own mind; and in the mist of tears
> I hid from him, and under running laughter
> . . . .
> Adown Titanic glooms of chasmèd fears
> From those strong feet, that followed, followed after.
> But with unhurrying chase
> and unperturbed pace,
> Deliberate speed, majestic instancy,
> They beat—and a Voice beat
> More instant than the Feet—
> 'All things betray thee, who betrayest Me'

And so, at last, the man asks:

> Is my gloom, after all,
> Shade of His hand, outstretched caressingly?
> 'Ah, fondest, blindest, weakest,
> I am He Whom thou seekest!
> Thou dravest love from thee, who dravest Me.'

So God gives us over to our sin and yet pursues us down the years until, like the prodigal, we find ourselves in the pigsty, eating the husks that the swine have mouthed and left. Then perchance we may remember the Father and find him there to welcome us home. "Only the suffering God can help" cried Bonhoeffer (*Letters and Papers, from Prison*; p. 197), and how true that is if the heart of the universe is love! The Cross on Calvary is an eruption into history of a love that will not let men go.

This suggests that the atonement on Calvary is an incarnation of God's eternal sin-bearing. He was forgiving men from the dawn of human history, and he is forgiving men still. He did not become the "Hound of heaven" on and after Calvary. That he has always been. His sin-bearing is brought to a focus in history, becomes incarnated there, but it is a reality always in the divine life. We cannot deny, therefore, the saving outreach of God in other moments of human history and indications of his liberating presence in other religions. Rather we must see such saving encounters brought to a climax and summed up in the sacrifice of the Christ. John Baillie, speaking of this, states that he cannot believe that any saving power manifested in man's religious history is not in some way related to the Christ-event. He continues: "I would . . . insist that the Eternal Christ who was made *flesh* in Jesus of Nazareth, and the Eternal Atonement which was made *event* on Calvary, were and are the source of every "saving process" which has at any time proved to be for the healing of the nations" (*The Sense of the Presence of God* [New York: Charles Scribners Sons, 1962], pp. 201-202. So we trace the Incarnation and the Cross down into God's eternal life and heart. Here is the source of that continuing activity in history which is ultimately fulfilled on Calvary. There, ἐφάπαξ "once for all,"the heart of eternity is laid bare in unique disclosure.

Here we are putting our finger on the most crucial point. The Incarnation and the Cross are necessary in a very real sense, for in them the living God met men where they have fixed their eyes. In the Christ-event, God took the guise of a man and confronted men in the market-place where they traffic and in the complex structure of human relationships. He was no longer a remote presence, hidden behind his creatures, guiding their history, speaking in their higher urges and noblest moments, touching their lives in times of religious insight, addressing them in prophetic words, pursuing them in diverse ways. Now he walked their common highways and met them in the press of life. Where they were taken up with possessing and acquiring, treating their fellows as "Its" to be exploited, he confronted them in his "Thou-ness" and called them back from sin to true personhood. In Jesus they met "the man for others." They met someone who treated others as "thous" and who accepted them in love, despite their selfishness and sin. Meeting him made them aware of their alienation and estrangement, and yet it also opened their lives to a forgiving, accepting love. It was not just a revelation of how a man could love and forgive. For many of them it was a disclosure of God. John Barnaby has written: "God's way of ending the separation between himself and sinful men was not to wait till men should return to him, but to go where they were *and to stay there*" (*Soundings*, ed. A. R. Vidler [Cambridge: The University Press, 1962], p. 229). In the Christ-event God gives historical actuality to that atoning activity which is eternally in his heart, and men face the reality of his grace wrought into their historical life. The eternal cross becomes incarnate. The Lamb that was slain on Calvary is the incarnation and historical actualization of the Lamb slain from the foundation of the world (Revelations 13:8).

When we speak of atonement we need to clarify one aspect of our preaching which often carries anachronistic undertones. Too frequently we use models derived from the past history of the Church which no longer speak to our contemporary scene. Aulen has made us aware of how strongly the early church employed the "Christus Victor" model; namely, the idea that, on the Cross, Christ battled with the devil and the powers of evil, winning the decisive victory and setting men free. There are dimensions of truth in this model which go back to the apostolic testimony. It provides, with its emphasis on man's liberation, a very vivid and preachable picture of the crucifixion. In addition, it makes clear that the Cross was no divine-human transaction but a divinely initiated act for us men and our salvation. Yet, despite *The Exorcist*, it is highly doubtful whether the mythology of the devil and his demons is the best way to describe the demonic forces in individual and social existence.

The model needs to be changed and linked with the sacrificial model which still speaks to modern man, provided we do not introduce the idea of transaction or repulsive language about "the blood." Christ sets us free by his vicarious sacrifice, but his is no sacrifice offered up to appease an angry God. God was in Christ reconciling the world to himself. In the Christ-event God was bringing his reconciling work to a climax in one supreme act of self-giving. The words in Hebrew and Greek which have so often been translated "propitiation" actually carry a different connotation. They are truly rendered "expiation." The equivalent verb means to expiate, to cover up. Hence we must not speak of Calvary as a propitiatory sacrifice, as the offering of satisfaction to an outraged deity. It is an expiatory sacrifice, which God himself provides, to cover our sin and remove our estrangement.

How do we preachers drive this truth home? Surely the sacrificial dimension of the Cross begins in that self-giving of God which initiates the Incarnation. The whole life of Jesus is one of self-giving. In this humanity God identified himself with our humanity to the point where he shared in our judgment. The God-man bore our sins in the sense that he shared in the consequences of our estrangement. What we do to one another we did in an extreme form to him; we drove him out of our world onto a cross. We rejected his self-giving love, but we could not abolish it. In his humanity God shared the consequences of our alienation until, on the Cross, he shared that alienation itself. In so doing, the Christ affirmed the moral nature of the universe and the righteousness of God. At the same time, at infinite cost, he offered us a forgiveness that we can never earn and which even the best of us does not deserve. The God-man experienced with a clarity that only the incarnate Son can experience the nature of sin and the reality of our judgment, and yet he could still speak the word of grace. He, being sinless, bore our sins in his own body on the tree. At infinite cost, God shows on Calvary what forgiveness means to him eternally. There he brings the eternal sacrifice and atonement to a historical consummation. The divine sin-bearing now stands unveiled in one supreme historical act. The expiatory view helps us, for, as Donald Baillie reminds us, "false ideas of propitiation obscured the truth that the Atonement is something within the life of God, wrought by God Himself, and applied by Him to men in every age" (*God Was in Christ,* p. 192).

So today, when the Gospel is preached, men cry: "He loved me and gave himself for me."For the Gospel is God's eternal message, the good news of his grace to sinful men. At infinite cost he has pursued humanity down the ages, until, in the fulness of time, he gave his Son. That historic act which consummates his self-giving in a disclosure event is an event in his life. And so it confronts men still through our preaching, becomes contemporaneous with them. History is still carried in the heart of God, but history is now different, for in one supreme event there has been a disclosure of the infinite grace which underlies all history and even creation. Pascal cried: "Jesus will be in agony even to the end of the world" (*Pensées,* quoted in Roger Hazelton, *Blaise Pascal: The Genius of His Thought* [Philadelphia: The Westminster Press, 1974], p. 137) The Christ toils up new Calvaries with the Cross upon his back.

This is the transforming power of the gospel., To know that we are loved to the point of death and beyond is to experience a grace that changes our lives. In *Crime and Punishment*, Dostoevski tells of such liberating grace. One character, Sonia, is driven to the streets by poverty and becomes a prostitute. The other, Raskolnikoff, has committed a horrible murder, driven to it by thwarted ambition. Both are spirits in prison, outcasts of society, whose only hope of liberation lies in death. They meet. Sonia has, despite her way of life, kept her New Testament. She opens it at the story of Lazarus and reads it to the miserable Raskolnikoff. She chooses the story because it is really her own stroy. She has been imprisoned in the tomb of sin, and like Lazarus she waits for the voice that wakes the dead. When she reads, "I am the Resurrection and the Life," she almost falters. But she reads on until she makes the confession of Martha her own: "Yea, Lord, I believe that Thou art the Christ, the Son of God, which should come into the world." For the Christ is risen, and because he lives we shall live also.

The Incarnation continues on earth, for the Risen Christ is born again in us as once he was born in Bethlehem. Do you remember John Betjeman's poem "Christmas"?

> And girls in slacks remember Dad,
> And oafish louts remember Mum,
> And sleepless children's hearts are glad,
> And Christmas-morning bells say 'come!'
> Even to shining ones who dwell
> Safe in the Dorchester Hotel
>
> And is it true? and is it true,
> This most tremendous tale of all,
> Seen in a stained-glass window's hue,
> A Baby in an ox's stall?
> The Maker of the stars and sea
> Becomes a Child on earth for me?
>
> No love that in a family dwells,
> No carolling in frosty air,
> Nor all the steeple-shaking bells
> Can with this single Truth compare—
> That God was Man in Palestine
> And lives today in Bread and Wine.
>
> *(John Betjeman's Collected Poems,*
> ed. the Earl of Birkenhead [London:
> John Murray, 1964], pp. 189-90).

3

The Preacher's Broad Canvas

A Redeemed World and
the Cosmic Christ

The Christian faith is world-affirming. Across the years, led by thinkers like Schleiermacher and Tillich, scholars have classified the world's religions under two major categories—the theological or ethical and the mystical or aesthetic. One other way of differentiating these two categories is to classify the first as world-affirming and the second as world-denying.

The first category includes Christianity, Judaism, Islam and Zoroastrianism. All are historical religions owing their origination to specific revelations given through historical figures—Jesus of Nazareth, the prophetic figures from Moses through Deutero-Isiah, the Rabbis of early Judaism, Mohammad and Zoroaster. All are world-affirming and correspondingly ethical in their teaching. The religious life must be lived out in the midst of human society and in the trafficking of this world. This world is regarded as a real stage in which man's relation to God is expressed in every-day relationships. Political, economic and social relationships are the milieu within which the moral aspect of these religions has to be expressed. There is no strong tendency to pantheism, for such religions regard man as a created being, other than, but responsibly related to, his Creator.

The second category includes the various forms of Hinduism and Buddhism and other minor oriental religions. These are world-denying, concerned with escape from this world and generally tending to deny its reality and regard it as illusion. The general viewpoint is that of pantheism, modified at times into a form of panentheism, and the customary form that such religion takes is that of mystical absorption in the deity.

In thus defining the category to which Christianity belongs as a world religion, we have already reemphasized points made earlier. However, we are now concerned with the relation of the Christian faith to the larger context of human society and natural environment in which the Christian life has to be lived. In so doing we must remind ourselves of what kind of life we preachers are presenting to our hearers as the liberated existence of the Christian person. We shall, however, commence once again with the Christ himself, and examine the relation of the historical disclosure in the Christ-event to this world in which our life has to be lived.

The Incarnate Eschaton and the Cosmic Christ

The New Testament witnesses always start with the historic disclosure. They do not start with cosmic speculation, but they move to this as a consequence of the insights of faith which are opened up in the disclosure itself.

First of all, they clearly identified Jesus with the consummation, the Kingdom of God to which the prophets looked forward in hope. That prophetic hope had been shaped in fragmentary form by the great classical prophets. Not one of them offered a complete pattern of the eschaton. The roots of the hope lay back in the divine promise to Abraham and the patriarchs, reconfirmed in the divine encounter with Moses. It was the promise of the land and the promise that, through the descendants of Abraham, divine blessing would reach out to all peoples of the earth. Another dimension was added in the covenant with David and the divine assurance that his succession was assured in his family line. This was taken up by prophets like Isaiah, Micah, and Jeremiah into the messianic hope—the hope that God would finally set an anointed descendant of David to preside over his restored people (Isaiah 9:6-7; 11:1ff.). Jeremiah and Ezekiel saw that such a restoration could only occur when God created a new spirit in the individual person, and so Jeremiah promised a new covenant which God would cut with the individual, forgiving men their sins and so transforming them within that they would seek God's will without outward constraint (Ezekiel 11:19; 36:26; Jeremiah 31:31ff.). Ezekiel looked for a healing stream that would flow from the altar of sacrifice, but Deutero-Isaiah went deeper and saw that the Messiah, and perhaps the restored remnant over which he ruled, might have to take the way of sacrifice to bring the nations back to God (Ezekiel 47; Isaiah 53). The thought that the remnant which survived God's purging judgment should be a missionary people, a saving remnant, is echoed often in Deutero-Isaiah (Isaiah 42: 6ff.; 49:6), but his especial insight comes in his very individualistic vision of the Suffering Servant through whose self-offering the nations would come to share in God's coming age. It was left for the apocalyptists to develop a new picture of a heavenly man sent to deliver God's people, a much more transcendent picture. Joel, who stands on the borderline between prophecy and apocalyptic, sees the spirit of God being poured out so that in the last days all men, young and old, shall share in the prophetic knowledge and vision and shall testify to that vision (Joel 2:28-29).

Here is the hope of Israel into the context of which Jesus was born. The New Testament Church saw him as the fulfillment of Israel's hopes, the coming of the end, the consummation of history to which the Old Testament prophets and saints looked forward. For us preachers, too, the Old Testament contains the word of God in promise, a partial disclosure that points to the Christ-event. Jesus Himself used the figures and images of the old covenant hope to describe his own ministry and to clothe his own thoughts. He could declare that in his casting out of demons, God's kingly power had been manifested in the midst (Luke 11:20). He could describe his own coming death in language which reflected the prophets' picture of the suffering servant. He could speak of his own coming death in terms of Jeremiah's new covenant, as he celebrated that death in symbolic form with his disciples (Mark 14:24). He never employed the description of himself as Messiah, even when Peter made his stumbling confession. Rather he hinted that he was not the kind of Messiah who would restore the Kingdom to Israel in the way men anticipated. His way was the way of death and suffering (Mark 8:17ff.). The disciples clearly did not understand this but hoped that he would be the conventionally pictured Messiah. For them his death shattered their dreams.

It was the Resurrection which awakened them to new insight, restored their faith in this mysterious Son of Man, brought to them the final assurance of a liberation and forgiveness which they had already experienced in his earthly ministry. God had raised him up, this Jesus (Acts 2:22-24; 3:15; 10:39-40). He had been declared Son of God with power by the resurrection from the dead (Roman 1:4). As he himself had said, the time had been filled full and the Kingdom of God was at hand (Mark 1:14). The new age, the age-to-come, had dawned, and the power of the coming Kingdom had been manifested in their midst. As John expressed it in his Gospel, they had received the gift of eternal life, the life of the age-to-come. Again, the vision of Joel had been actualized and the Spirit of God had been poured forth (Acts 3:15ff.). The followers of Jesus found new life in the Risen Christ, for they received the gift of his continuing presence in his Spirit. They were in Christ, a new creation, activated by his love. The eschaton had been incarnated in Jesus, and the final consummation was in process. They were living in the days of the Son of Man, the dawning of the final Day.

Here the Christian faith differs from the Old Testament hope. For the Old Testament men, the age-to-come would mean the end of this present order, but, for the apostolic witnesses, the age-to-come had supervened on this present evil age in such a way that the latter still continued. So the Christians were those upon whom the ends of the ages had come, the ages overlapped (Corinthians 10:11). They are in Christ and also in the flesh, in the Spirit but also on Patmos. They live, yet not they, but Christ lives in them, for the presence of Christ's Spirit within is a guarantee of their future inheritance; they are already sampling that full life which comes at the End. (Ephesians 1:13-14). They have eternal life, here and now (John 3:15; 17:3).

Thus the Christ-event is the end before the end. In this disclosure God's ultimate purpose for the universe is unveiled. The final consummation will be the final unveiling of what is disclosed in the midst of history in the life, death and resurrection of Jesus of Nazareth. He is the incarnate eschaton, the assurance of God's ultimate triumph. The Christian, because he is a new creation in Christ, knows that though his outward man perishes, his inward man is being daily renewed; he already participates in the future age (2Corthinians 4:16). In Christ the ultimate future has become a present reality.

The apostolic witnesses looked, not only to the future, but also to the past and, in so doing, into the depth of eternity. Since, for them, God had spoken his final Word of redemption in Jesus, the incarnate Word, they moved in their inspired reflection back to the moment of creation. If the Christ is sufficient to liberate the human heart, he must have created the human heart. This was the way Deutero-Isaiah had moved—if Yahweh could shape nature and make a way through the wilderness for his liberated people, he must be the creator of nature. The redeeming God is the creating God. The long travail of Israel's history, as the elected and covenanted people of God, had begun when God had created the world as the scene for the actualization of his purpose. Now, in the Christ-event, the divine fulfillment of that purpose had taken place in veiled form. The new age had come into being by this new and redemptive mighty act of God in Jesus. A new creation was taking place, and a new people of God was being constituted. Surely, then, the author and agent of the new creation must be the author and agent of the old creation. So the New Testament men moved in inspired logic from a redeeming Christ to a creating Christ. But that meant that God's coming in the Christ-event would involve the Christ in a divine pre-existence. The "Son of God" became God the Son, the Word, the Cosmic Christ, in his divine dimension.

The mental atmosphere was ready for the clothing of this insight which carried the Christ down into the depths of eternity and back along the history of the race to the moment of creation. Had not God, in the Hebrew traditions, created the world by his uttered word? The divine intention had taken concrete form in the word. As such it was flung into the chaos, and cosmos came into being. It initiated a creative movement. Furthermore, the wise men had personified the divine wisdom as enshrining the divine plan and as active agent alongside of God in the creative process (Proverbs 8:22-31; Exodus 24; Wisdom of Soloman 7:25ff.). And the divine Wisdom and divine Word were almost identical. The Word is the divine Wisdom given concrete form. It describes the Wisdom of God in action. And in Christ the Wisdom of God is present (1 Corinthians 1:24, 30). Again, the Greeks (Heraclitus and the Stoics, for example) were speaking of the Logos as the divine principle of rationality in the universe, the embodiment of the divine reason, in which the human reason participated. The great Jewish Hellenist in Alexandria, Philo, was seeking to assimilate the Word/Wisdom concepts to the Logos idea. In this atmosphere, the thought of the preexistent Christ found its garb.

Paul, the anonymous author of the Epistle to the Hebrews, and John all manifest this concern to present the Christ in his pre-existent and cosmic glory. (Colossians 1:11-16; Hebrew 1:1-2; John 1:1-14). He who stands at the End, summing up all things in himself, stands also at the beginning, initiating the whole creative process. So the incarnation is set in a cosmic as well as a historical framework. We see this in the Kenotic hymn of Philippians 2:6-11. It begins with the Cosmic Christ who is in the form of God. The movement of self-emptying leads through the exaltation to the heavenly glory. The Christ becomes the one before whom all knees shall bow, and so the historical movement achieves its eschatological objective, and the cosmic backdrop is complete. The Prologue to the Gospel of John uses the Logos concept and represents the Christ as the preexistent Word through whom all things come into being. The historical movement proceeds with the Cosmic Christ as the general enlightener of men's minds, as the specific agent of the revelation through the prophets who are born of the will of God, and reaches its climax in the Incarnate Presence. Here too the preexistence is stressed. Paul's vision in Colossians goes further, for he sees the Cosmic Christ, the divine Son, not only as the agent of creation but as the integrating principle of the universe. He not only brings the cosmos into being, but, like the Greek Logos, he holds it together. The description of the historical life brings the emphasis that the fullness of God dwelt in him in bodily form (see Colossians 2:9), that is, under human conditions. The eschatalogical and cosmic motif provides the final element in the cosmic framework. We are told that the Christ will ultimately accomplish a cosmic reconciliation, bring all things in heaven and on earth into a harmonious whole (Colossians 1:20). In Ephesians 1:9-10, the divine objective in the cosmic process is again emphasized. God intends in the final consummation ("the fullness of time") to unite all things, things *in heaven* and things on earth, in Christ.

There is no Trinitarian speculation here. but there is the affirmation that, in the Christ-event, men have apprehended the mind and will of God. They have experienced his redemptive activity and known that his fullness dwells within the limitations of a human life. And they have dared to believe that the Christ towers beyond those limitations and human conditioning up into the transcendent heights of deity. He is in some way God. He transcends this cosmos even though he stooped to accept the historical conditions of our humanity.

What all this demands of us is a much more Christocentric emphasis in our preaching. We need to relate the Christ to the universe, to nature and the processes which science studies, to history and the life of human societies, to culture and the values which give meaning to human existence, to man's religions and the age-old search for God. So often we make our Christ too small. In days when television and popular journals are painting a big canvas, we need to set our Christian faith in such a framework. We cannot be satisfied with a parochial picture of Jesus as the Savior of individual men only, or with a Gospel which is simply concerned to save people from hell and get them on the way to heaven. The disclosure of the Christ-event does have something to say about the scientific understanding of our world and of life, about the historical events and crises which beset contemporary society, about the tensions and values which are manifested in contemporary culture. You may remember Alice Meynell's poem:

But not a star of all
The innumerable host of stars has heard
How he administered this terrestrial ball
Our race has kept their Lord's entrusted Word.
Nor, in our little day,
May His devices with the heavens be guessed,
His pilgrimage to thread the Milky Way
Or his bestowal there be manifest.
But in the eternities,
Doubtless we shall compare together, hear
A million alien Gospels, in what guise
He trod the Pleiades, the Lyre, the Bear.
O, be prepared, my soul!
To read the inconceivable, to scan
The million forms of God those stars unroll
When, in our turn, we show to them a Man.

(Alice Meynell, "Christ in the Universe," cited in John Baille's *A Diary of Readings* [New York: Charles Scribner's Sons, 1955], Day 130). This poem brings us to the first issue that we need to examine

The Unfinished Universe and the Unveiling of the Sons of God

The Hebrew mind retained enough of the primitive animistic philosophy to think of the whole world as alive and bound together in a network of psychic relationships. Every entity was, to its own degree, related and responsive to other entities. The relationships of nature could even be described by the concept of covenant which applied particularly at the human level. Thus God had a covenant with nature and with its various "kinds" and appointed the statutes or decrees which governed their life. He called them into being and gave them life, and he ordained their "life-style." Hosea has a vivid picture of how Jezreel is fed. He pictures a chain of psychic responses stretching from God to the heavens with their rain, to the earth with its fertility, to the grains with their food-potential, to the hungry citizens of Jezreel (Hosea 2:21-22). Thus nature was quasi-independent. It had a life of its own and followed its appointed course. This was true of the sun and moon as well as of terrestrial entities (Psalms 19:1-7; Jeremiah 8:6, 7; 31:35).

Man must respect the life of nature, whether it be his beast of burden (Proverbs 12:10) or his field, by leaving it fallow one year in seven, or his grain, by leaving a corner unreaped. He also was within a covenant structure with nature. The wild animals could rove freely because they had no covenant with man, but the domestic animals had such a covenant, and man must respect its obligations (Jeremiah 41:4). Man was given dominion over the lower orders of nature, but always under God. He was a divinely ordained steward, for it was God who had put all things in subjection under his feet (Genesis 1:26-31; Psalms 8:5-9).

Indeed, God had a universal covenant with men and nature in which he promised to preserve the regularity of nature despite the waywardness of man Genesis 9:8-17). Here we note another aspect of man's relationship to his natural environment. For man was bound to God and to nature in a kind of triangular covenant relationship, and when his relationship to God went wrong, his relationship to nature went wrong too. So in the Fall story of Genesis 3, man becomes estranged from God only to find himself estranged also from nature, which hits back at him with thorns and thistles. The potential Garden of God becomes a wilderness. This is one aspect of the judgment on sinful humanity, and it is significant that the prophets saw the wrath of God manifested in the return of the desert or of the chaos out of which God had first called forth his ordered world, the cosmos.

Today we are becoming increasingly aware of the kind of insight which the biblical writers possessed. We have long since left their primitive animism behind. We have learned more and more to control and subdue our natural environment. Science is within the divine intention for man. We preachers must beware of attacking science and ignoring its discoveries. At the same time, we need to make our people aware of its limitations and to attack the naturalism which it so often nourishes. For it is easy for the modern scientist, because his methods are so successful, to believe that the sole reality is that with which science deals. Any idea of transcendence in the case of personal self-transcendence, and still more in the realm of religion, must be denied. To speak of a transcendent deity or of the supernatural is to speak nonsense. There is no supernature. Nature is all that is. Its physical energies and biological urges suffice to account for the world and for man himself.

But while we must reject naturalism, we need to make our people aware of how the Christian faith reinforces many of the findings which science provides, and how it supplies a deeper understanding of our world. We may reject the biblical animism as a reflection of its contemporary culture, but, in its own way, science is reminding us of the interrelatedness of our world. There is evidence of a balanced and ordered regularity within the operations of nature. It is not perfect, but it is present. We think of the mysterious chemical fitness of the natural environment to produce life. We are very aware of the balanced ecosystems—the oxygen, water and nitrogen cycles without which life would not be possible; the ecological pyramid with its food chains upon which the survival of all living things depends. The balance of nature would seem to require that herbivores become the prey of carnivores. And ultimately comes man, carnivorous and herbivorous, bound up with nature, as we are increasingly aware. Our modern ecological concern would be no surprise to the Hebrews, however much our modern science and technology would leave them bewildered.

The contemporary ideas of eco-justice are as old as the revelation to which the Bible bears witness. We are under a covenanted responsibility to nature because we are in covenant relationship to God. God has created us to be his stewards. Because we have rejected his plan, we face an ecological crisis in which nature is hitting back at us. The irresponsible application of scientific discovery and the harnessing of our technological skills to the exploitation of our natural environment have brought us to the edge of self-destruction. Here, indeed, is one indication that man destroys himself by sin and thus brings about his own judgment in a moral universe.

The biblical creation stories share a significant insight with the creation myths of other religions. The Creator began with chaos and shaped it into cosmos. The Biblical stories describe the chaos variously as formless void, darkness, the deep, or the desert. One does not have to be an obscurantist or a literalist to see here a tacit understanding of the divine activity. It is significant that modern science, in the generally accepted "big-bang" theory, envisages a tremendous explosion of energy out of which the chemical elements and their increasingly complex combinations were formed until, on the planet earth, life and ultimately man emerged.

Modern science is making us increasingly aware of the chaotic, contingent, random aspects of our world. The atomic scientist generally agrees that there is an acausal structure in the basic stuff of the universe. He postulates an element of indeterminancy in the fundamental units of physical energy, and he speaks of probability, not certainty. At the higher level, the physicist reminds us that all our experimental scientific laws are statistical averages, concerned with probabilities, not certainties. Again, the biologist offers an understanding of the evolutionary process which speaks of random mutations operated upon by natural selection, so that only the fittest survive. Everywhere contingency and randomness are present, and from one point of view, the universe might appear to be the dicing table of the gods.

This is an unfinished universe. Despite its orderliness and regularity, with which science is concerned, within this framework the chaotic aspect is evident. Nature has its warring systems and changing seasons, its hurricanes and tornadoes, its earthquakes and tidal waves, its cancers and malformed genetic structures. The balance and order of nature are not perfect. It has dimensions of rape and cruelty, although often we humans are prone to read our own feelings into the lower creatures. Tennyson saw nature as "red in tooth and claw with ravin'." The waste associated with the proliferation of offspring presented a challenge to his religious faith. He wrote:

> Are God and Nature then at strife,
>   That Nature lends such evil dreams?
>   So careful of the type she seems,
> So careless of the single life;
>
> That, I considering everywhere
>   Her secret meaning in her deeds,
>   And finding that of fifty seeds,
> She often brings but one to bear,
>
> I falter where I firmly trod
>   And falling with my weight of cares

Upon the great world's altar stairs
That slope thro' darkness up to God,
I stretch lame hands of faith, and grope,
. . . .
And faintly trust the larger hope.
(Alfred, Lord Tennyson, *In Memoriam*, LV).

Tennyson did not see the background of cooperation of which scientists remind us. Indeed, the biological understanding of evolution today makes much more of this than did Tennyson's contemporaries, especially T. H. Huxley.

Tennyson's point, however, still remains, because the problem of natural evil—from tornadoes to cancers, and from earthquakes to mongoloids—still faces us preachers and perplexes our hearers. The presence of evil in our world is a mystery with which the Christian faith has to wrestle and which can raise a real barrier to belief.

Since much of natural evil arises from the unfinished nature of the universe and not just from man's sinful mishandling of his world, it is good that we should seek for some partial light upon the mystery which it presents. For one thing, we need to remember that growth comes through challenge, so that the whole process of nature with its developing life-forms requires opposition and resistance. Life develops by tension and polarities. The storm makes the tree grow a deeper root. The living creatures develop their capacities in the struggle for existence. So, if this is a world in the making, and if creation is a progressive movement towards the emergence of man, as Christians believe, then the warring systems and random elements are necessary for creative development, a dimension of the divine purpose.

They are also a part of the price that God is prepared to pay to create men with the gift of freedom. For in the second place, the mingling of contingency with order makes it possible for man to be a free being and yet for the universe to have regularity and consistency. We have already emphasized the mystery of human freedom and the failure of the sciences to penetrate its inner depths by treating it as a soluble problem. It is not a problem, but a mystery. Now, if such freedom is the ultimate objective of the process, we begin to see a rationale in the unfinished state of the universe. Had the universe been created along rigidly determined lines and with a rigorously law-bound structure, God would have produced automata, not free men. The world is in process and unfinished in order that, out of it, man may emerge with his freedom, and so that there may be an area in which he will be free to exercise his own creativity. Understood in the light of the divine disclosure in the Christ-event, God was concerned to share his own freedom with created beings in order that they might respond in love to their Creator and also be co-creators with him in the completion of his purpose. From such a viewpoint, the unfinished nature of the universe and its aspect of randomness would seem to be expected.

Yet the presence of such chaos in his world and the suffering it entails may well be part of God's eternal cross. However much the unfinished nature of the universe and its accompanying contingency may serve the divine purpose, a God of love can 'let it be' only at a cost. The creation of a world like this points to Calvary and the Christ-event as much as does man's misuse of his freedom. The Cosmic Christ who is the agent of creation bears the cost of its redemption. This too is part of the Cross in the heart of God.

This brings us, finally, to the natural process itself and the issue of evolution. (On this section see E. C. Rust, *Science and Faith* [New York: Oxford University Press, 1967], pp. 165ff.) Again we preachers face difficulties, and yet must not evade them if the Christian faith is to be made intelligible to secular man. We have already suggested that we must not absolutize the cultural outlook of the biblical writers and therefore must not take their stories literally. With two stories of creation we should have difficulty here, in any case! The stories, however, carry revelatory insight. The writers express in the pre-scientific world structure of their day the world view of the biblical faith. By world view we mean the revealed awareness of a transcendent God and his creative purpose. When Julian Huxley (*Evolution in Action* [New York: Harper & Brothers, 1953]), the naturalistic thinker, can state that "the primacy of human personality . . . is a *fact* of evolution," modern man cannot cavil with the Christian affirmation that the emergence of man is central in the divine creative purpose. This is what both the creation stories affirm, and this is finally confirmed in the Christian conviction that the humanity of Jesus is the historicity of God.

Alongside their insights into chaos, the creation stories see that creation has a history. It is a process Further, alongside their emphasis on God's transcendence, his otherness from his creation, they see his immanence. In Gen. 1 especially, God projects himself creatively into the developing process through his uttered Word and also becomes active within it through the presence of his Spirit.

This suggests that the whole process of evolution needs a deeper dimension of understanding than the mechanism with which biological science is concerned. The tendency to reduce biology to biochemistry and biophysics is symptomatic of the reductionism which pervades the scientific approach to reality. An explanation in terms of the laws of physics and chemistry is regarded as sufficient. But A. N. Whitehead (*Science and the Modern World* [Cambridge: Cambridge University Press, 1932]) and Michael Polanyi (*Personal Knowledge* [Chicago: University of Chicago Press, 1958], passim), along with many others, have been reminding us that science has so majored on the analytic approach that it has ignored the synthetic approach to reality. It has ignored the holistic view of reality which is very evident in the Hebrew way of thinking. A whole is more than the sum of its parts. We can analyze scientifically the parts which compose a living whole. But, once we have taken Humpty Dumpty to pieces, we cannot put him together again. For a living whole is not just an aggregation of a number of parts. It is an organization of those parts into a meaningful whole. It is an organism. The internal organization of an organism is the indication of a mysterious interrelatedness which is lost when science isolates the parts and treats them as objects of physical and chemical analysis. This is one example of the abstract approach of science. Whitehead has called this "the fallacy of misplaced concreteness" (*Science and the Modern World*, pp. 72-73), the method of cutting living reality up into lumps of matter separated in space and moving in time and then replacing the mysterious interrelatedness by mechanistic causation. Polanyi points out (*The Tacit Dimension* [Garden City NY: Doubleday & Co., 1967], pp. 38ff.) that we do not understand a machine when we have complete knowledge of the physics and chemistry of its parts. For the machine is more than the parts. It is the parts organized and related to serve a certain purpose, and to understand the machine we must understand the principle underlying its organization. So a living whole has a higher law than the laws of physics and chemistry which hold for its parts. The latter laws are transcended by the law which applies to the organizing principle of the whole. This principle sets boundary conditions to limit the operations of the lower laws, and the operation of the living whole is not to be explained in terms of those lower laws. The holistic principle directs the parts with their lower laws to serve its purpose. We are, in this way, left with a heirarchy of levels in nature, stretching from the inanimate through the animate and the conscious to self-consciousness in man. The fact that man emerges at the end suggests that there is an overall organizing principle directing the whole process. Did not God's Spirit brood over the deep?

Most of what we have said above cannot be offered to our hearers, but we can help them to accept an evolutionary process and see it as the creative activity of the living God. Charles Raven (*The Creator Spirit* [London: Martin Hopkenson & Co., 1927]), William Temple (*Nature, Man, and God* [London: Macmillan & Co., 1934]), and Teilhard de Chardin (*The Phenomenon of Man* [New York: Harper & Row, 1959]) have, each in his own way, offered a viable approach to evolution as a creative process. Probably Teilhard's is the most attractive, although it is overly optimistic and has a very inadequate understanding of the depth of sin and evil. As mystic visionary and anthropologist, he has much to offer us, and we shall make use of his thought, blending it with the insights of the other thinkers and avoiding his peculiar terminology.

Since, in man, the process has become conscious of itself, producing a being who can understand the process and to some degree determine its future development, we might expect that man's rational mind and self-conscious spirit are rooted back in the very beginning of the process. Further, we might expect that human reason is able to grasp the process scientifically because there is a corresponding rational reality within and guiding the whole process. As Tillich would put it, the *logos* in man is analogous to the divine *logos*. Temple holds that man's scientific knowledge points to immanent mind throughout the process. Raven speaks of the immanent directing presence of the Creator Spirit. Teilhard finds an immanent driving principle (or entelechy) which drives the process forward. He paints a picture of God as the eternal lure who ever draws the process towards himself. God is the Omega Point, and the whole creative process will find its consummation by being gathered into him.

We may picture God as creating the world so that all the potencies and powers necessary for its ultimate perfection are already nascent in its origination. Whatever energy is, it must not be thought of solely in physical terms. Rather, potential within it are the possibilities of mind or consciousness and spirit or self-consciousness. The Cosmic Christ, the creative Word, guides the process through the immanent activity of the Spirit, so that, with the increasing complexity at the physical level, living wholes begin to form. Such wholes successively manifest the organizing principles which we associate with life, mind, and human spirit. Thus, a hierarchy of levels, from the lowest amoeba to man with his self-transcendence and freedom, emerges within the process in developmental order. At the same time, the process manifests those contingent aspects which God "lets be" so that finite human spirits may act in freedom. The emergence of these successive levels is a creative surge forward in the process. Teilhard likens it to a change of state when supersaturation occurs. For us it is sufficient to see the continuing immanent creative activity of the Spirit. New levels of existence emerge in moments of creative upheaval. What was potential in energy is actualized, when conditions are ripe for its emergence.

With man the process reaches its climax on this planet. Now he extends his presence and influence all over the planet. He also is in a position to control the direction of the process within limits set by the Creator. Included in such limits are the movements of self-destruction which sinful humanity brings on itself by its misuses of its freedom. Yet the movement of evolution is now more in the social realm than in the physical. The human spirit is groping toward its final destiny, constrained by the presence of the Creator Spirit. The history of nature has given precedence to the history of humanity.

The Cosmic Christ who has been guiding the whole process creatively through his Spirit now assumes his role as the Incarnate Eschaton. In the midst of human history, the Christ-event releases, in fuller measure, the liberating activity of God. In his life, death and resurrection, the powers of the age to come are released in this present evil age. Believers receive in promise an experience of the future consummation; they are liberated to enjoy the liberty of the sons of God; they are dowered with eternal life.

Nature and the world still go on, and nature is not to be stripped away and abolished even in the final consummation. It is now subject to corruption and decay. So Paul sees it in Rom. 8:19ff. It is subject to frustration. Suffering and tragedy are written across its face, reflecting man's alienation from God and from nature. It is unfinished, and the chaotic elements ever lurk on its boundary. It groans and travails along with us, waiting for its own deliverance. Paul Tillich describes Paul's vision as a dream, but adds that "it contains a profound truth: man and nature belong together in their created glory, in their tragedy, and in their salvation" *(The Shaking of the Foundations* [New York: Charles Scribner's Sons, 1948] p. 83). Our hope is cosmic. Nature has an ultimate meaning for God. It has its contributions to make in God's perfected purpose, and he plans a resurrection for the universe. The universe too strains forward eagerly for the final unveiling of the sons of God. But already in Christ that unveiling is taking place. This means that the Church has a responsibility for establishing right relations with the natural order. In this way it may contribute to the final coming of the Christ, when he will sum up all things in himself.

In one sense the Resurrection of Jesus initiates a new humanity. It is the final stage in the evolutionary process. Like the other stages it comes by a creative upheaval, and its pattern is one of death and resurrection. The Christian has to die to the old man, with and in Christ, and be raised to the new. Liberation from sin means beings raised to newness of life. Is that pattern true also of the universe? Maybe the second Law of Thermodynamics, with its presaged "heat death" of the universe, is the physical side of the pattern! So the Seer of Revelation sees a *new* heaven and a *new* earth in which righteousness dwells (Revelation 21:1).

To speak of the universe in this way is to dwarf man (Ps. 8), and yet the Incarnation places man right in the center of this infinite universe. In becoming man, the Christ not only affirmed man, he affirmed nature and the universe. The whole cosmos is brought to a focus in the Incarnation. Yet its ultimate redemption is not just for the sake of man—it has its own ultimate meaning. God rejoiced in it on the morn of creation, not merely because it should be a habitat for man made in his image, but also because it had its own life and reflected back to him some facets of that outpoured love which he lavished on his world.

And if there be life on other planets, the Christ will function there, for he will sum up the whole universe in the final consummation. Eric Mascall faces the possibility that there may be "somewhere in the universe rational beings other than man." He concludes his discussion of the possibility of their being fallen by declaring that he "cannot see any conclusive theological objection to the view that the divine Word may have become incarnate in other rational species than our own" (E. Mascall, *Christian Theology and Natural Science*, [New York: The Ronald Press Co., 1956], p. 44). Wherever creation exists, there redemption will operate. The Christ, through whom all things came to be, will finally become incarnated in the whole process, and God will be all in all.

What the Christ has brought into being, he will also liberate, and in the center there will be the unveiling of the sons of God—from planet earth and perhaps from elsewhere!

The Resurrected Humanity and the Drama of History

Our hearers often keep a firm line to separate the sacred from the secular, especially in their thinking. They somehow do not expect that what they hear from the pulpit has any direct relevance to what is happening in the historical scene, what they will read about in the voluminous Sunday newspaper or see and hear on the TV news. Secular news reports do not often mention God, unless some piece of religious scandal is available. Religion is concerned with heaven and hell and individual morality, but the Christian faith must not interfere in areas like politics, social problems and international relationships. Such areas do not come under its aegis. In part, we preachers are to blame, for so often we have kept silent over big social issues and concentrated on a narrow understanding of evangelism. We have forgotten that the Church is the living conscience of the community. We have not offered our people a big enough canvas on which to present our faith. That God is active on the large scene of human history is mentioned rarely, and often then only in passing.

In 1652, when Cromwell was ruling in England and there was a war with Holland, the great Puritan divine, John Owen, preached before Parliament. Things were going badly in the war, and Owen said some significant words: "You take counsel with one another. You hearken unto men with a repute of wisdom, and all this doth but increase your trouble. You do but more and more entangle and disquiet your own spirits. God stands by, and says, 'I am wise also,' but very little notice is taken of him." More than ever Owen's words need to ring through the halls of government and the homes of men.

Since our faith is world-affirming and centers in the Incarnation, the very historicity of God himself, this is the note that the Christian preacher ought to be sounding. The Christ-event is history, but then the background of that event, the long historical travail of the Jewish people from Moses onward, is also concerned with a God who acts in history. The two Isaiahs emphasized this in characteristic ways. Isaiah of Jerusalem saw God acting in judgment through historical movements. The invasion of Judah by Assyria served God's purpose, even though the King of Assyria had no such thought. The latter was bent on plunder and the extension of his dominions. In his arrogance the Assyrian conqueror saw himself as the lord of history. Yet he was only a rod in God's hand, powerless if God's hand should let it fall. His plans served God's purpose of judgment on Israel, and when that purpose had been accomplished, he too would succumb to the divine judgment. God would kindle a burning like that of a fire under Assyria's glory, for he is the "Lord of hosts," the God who controls the heavenly bodies and directs the forces of history in spite of themselves. (Isaiah 10:12-16).

We have already seen that God's judgment is a historical movement in which man's individual and corporate sins are self-distructive. Societies set certain historical movements in motion which come back on them in judgment. Early in his Protestant leadership, Luther published a tract giving an exposition of the Magnificat. Reflecting on the pride and fate of great empires and civilizations, he held that not power but the abuse of the power is what is wrong. He wrote, "For while the earth remains authority, rule, power. . .must needs remain. But God will not suffer men to abuse them. He puts down one Kingdom and exalts another: increases one people and destroys another: as he did with Assyria, Babylon, Greece and Rome though they thought they should sit in their seats forever." So, Luther pointed out, they put themselves up in their power alone, stretching their authority and arrogantly expanding their sway. But this inflation, balloon like, brings about their destruction. For like a great bubble they suddenly burst. "God pricks the bubble and it is all over," says Luther. (cited in E. G. Rupp, *The Righteousness of God* [London: Hodder and Stoughton, 1953], p. 11).

God pricks the bubble by the processes of history. Sometimes the systems become so corrupt that they burst from within. As A. J. Toynbee has pointed out, when in its arrogance a civilization rests back upon its seeming supremacy and power, it begins to fall apart within. The challenge of an opposing power is no longer there to unite the people, for the empire has mastered its historical environment. With no such unifying catalyst, warring groups and factions assert themselves and the civilization disintegrates from within. Small and large nations around, who have gone in fear, find that the whole is a hollow sham. Toynbee comments that "the story turns out to be a simple illustration of the theme that 'the wages of Sin is Death.' " (A. J. Toynbee, *A Study of History*, vol. 5 [New York: Oxford University Press, 1946], p. 16). At other times, the bubble is pricked when some superior military force intervenes. God is at work in history. His wrath is operative. But he is using the movements of history to achieve his purpose. Always he is a hidden God, hidden behind his creatures. I like Luther's expression when he describes the creatures as the *larvae* of God. By this Luther means that God is always active in his creation, and that his creatures are "masks" or *larvae* behind which he hides while dealing with his world. Incomplete in themselves, they carry an echo of God who uses them and yet hides behind them.

God's constraining pressure is there, but finally it is the pressure of suffering, redeeming love. So the prophets see judgment as always a call to repentence, as if God in his mercy is always waiting for the prodigal to come home. Deutero-Isaiah emphasized this facet of the divine activity. He celebrated God as Creator and Redeemer, delivering his people from exile as once he had brought them up out of Egypt, using nature to facilitate their return, and making possible for them a new exodus. So the prophetic message changes from one of doom to one of comfort, from judgment to redemption. The most significant oracles of Deutero-Isaiah are to be found in the "Servant Songs." Here the prophet paints a picture of God's servant through whose sufferings all nations will be brought near. Although the servant appears to be a corporate figure representing the faithful of the restored nation, the songs increasingly point to a more individual picture. In chapter 53 the servant, whose sufferings are a sacrifice for the peoples, becomes an eschatological figure, a kind of suffering messianic image. It is a picture actualized in the Christ-event, a picture of a divine activity in which indentification with sinners in their judgment can become an actualization of divine grace.

We are presented with a picture of the constraining pressure of divine love as the background of history. God reigns, but he reigns from a Cross. His omnipotence is the omnipotence of love. It is the power of a restraint, which sustains history and bears the sin of historical man in the divine heart. Such a God is, as John Macquarrie put it, a God who lets be. World History, as von Ranke saw, is world-judgment—*Weltgeschichte ist weltgericht.* God gives men and their social structures over to the sin of their hearts and thus to their own self-destruction. Yet the last word is not judgment but love, not death but life, for at the heart of history there is a cross.

Dr. Laws, the missionary to Africa in the early days of this century, once told of an African landscape in which trees were all inclined from a certain direction, shall we say from the west. He could not account for this, however, since the gales and the tempests blew from the east. If the winds had been the determining factors in the inclination of the tree trunks, then the inclination should have been in the opposite direction to its actual setting.Then Laws discovered that the steady prevailing winds blew from the west. The gales and tempests only blew with their ferocious blast for a time. When they had ceased, the breezes reasserted themselves, and their steady pressure determined the inclination of the tree trunks. I like to think of God's activity in history in this way. He who transcends history is yet immanent in history, hidden though he may be. The Christ-event is simply God bringing his universal presence and activity to a focus. As Bonhoeffer put it, "God is 'beyond in the midst of life."

Medieval art made a great step forward when it discovered perspective. Flat pictures began to manifest depth. So it was with history in the Christ-event. It was given depth and perspective. His life, death and resurrection disclosed the transcendent God and yet revealed him as immanent in history, dynamic and active, creating and redeeming. It was the Resurrection of Jesus which finally opened men's eyes and transformed his death on the Cross from a martyr's death to a redeeming sacrifice, from a revelation of the abysmal depths of human sin and cruelty to a disclosure of a grace beyond man's deserving. The Resurrection set the seal upon the life and death of Jesus, confirming their disclosure and affirming the activity in them, and therefore in history, of a loving and gracious Presence. The transcendent God was also immanent; he was the beyond in the midst.

We need to ponder this Resurrection event and to emphasize it in our preaching. It is the event which changed the course of history. Without it the Christ-event would have been incomplete and its disclosure, if any, of little redemptive significance. The evidence of the four Gospels and of Paul points to an event that can be dated within certain limits, but it is difficult to paint a picture of the actual happening. An empty tomb; appearances to Peter, to Paul, to the disciples, to the women; indications that the physical appearance of Jesus did not prevent his passage through closed doors; sudden appearances and disappearances as a physical presence—all present problems, quite apart from the fact that the evidential data manifests inconsistencies. Yet we are left with the conviction that the Christ had been raised in bodily form and had been a presence empirically observable by his followers. There was an extraordinary happening, but it was also a disclosure event. And what really matters is that disclosure! God had said "Yes" to Jesus and to his sacrifice. He had been declared the Son of God with power by the resurrection from the dead. A new age had dawned. The hymns, confessions and sermons of the early Church cannot be understood without the Resurrection, nor, indeed, can the very existence of the Church itself. Here we face a miracle that *is* a miracle, a happening which defies all the normal regularities of nature, a happening which becomes a redemptive event, a miraculous act of God.

We have less difficulty in understanding such an occurrence if we remember that Jesus was the incarnate eschaton. The end-time, the consummation, had supervened upon the normal movement of human history. The powers of the age to come had been released in this life. Forces that would function when the present structures had run their course had taken over in the Resurrection event. In miniature and yet in the mightiest of all mighty acts, the consummation was already present. What could only happen at the end was already taking place when God raised Jesus from the dead. The abrogation of the normal processes of this age in this Resurrection-event was a part of the disclosure. It bore testimony to the fact that the future had become present and the Kingdom of God had dawned with saving power.

History could never be the same again. Like some celestial Samson, the Christ had come out of Gaza carrying the gates upon his shoulders. He had led captivity captive and brought life and immortality to light. He liberated men from their prison house of sin and created a new humanity. His death and resurrection became the pattern for entrance into the age to come. He had created a new exodus and brought into being a new people of God.

And so in the midst of this world, there are the citizens of the world-to-come. The mystery of the Incarnation is continued down through history in the mystery of the church. The apostolic witnesses employ various models or images by which to describe the Church. It is the Body of Christ, the on-going of the Incarnation, the instrument of the Risen Christ through his Spirit, the central medium of his activity in history. It is the People of God, created by the new exodus of the death and resurrection of the Christ and bound to God by the new covenant which he had made possible. Did not Jesus choose twelve disciples symbolic of the recreation of the old Israel with its twelve tribes? So the Church is the new Israel. It is the new creation made possible by the sacrifice of Christ. It is a building with Jesus Christ as the chief cornerstone, to be indwelt by God in the Spirit. It is the resurrected humanity, the company of those who by faith in and commitment to the Christ have died with him and been raised with him to newness of life.

The Church is, indeed, bound up with the Resurrection and with Pentecost, with the risen Christ and with his continuing immanent presence in his Spirit. It is the community of the Age-to-Come, and in it the powers of that age are being released. The grace of God is active in its midst, creating a fellowship of love. For the relationships within this new humanity are characterized by the new kind of self-giving love which was manifested in Christ. It is a love that spends itself, a love that loves the unlovely and makes them worthwhile by loving them, a love that recreates. It is *agape*, and the Church had to coin this word to describe it, for the other available Greek words could not describe this unique love which was disclosed in the Christ-event. To be redeemed is to be set free to love and serve as Christ loved and served. It means to enter into a fellowship, for such love transforms our relationships and binds us all together around the foot of Calvary. God's love flows out from Christ and his cross into our lives and welds us together into a fellowship of love. Committed to the Christ whose love has liberated us, we are now constrained by that love to love our brothers and follow Christ's path of self-sacrifice. As Bonhoeffer put it, the Christian is one in whom the Christ is forming his form again.

The first thing which the Church has contributed to history is, of course, the Gospel of grace. The Church is a witnessing community, witnessing to the Christ-event and the pardoning love for sinful men which is disclosed in Jesus of Nazareth. It seeks to evoke faith in Christ, and it offers men the grace which liberates them from the prison-house of sin. Once the Church ceases to propagate the Gospel and to forsake the foolishness of preaching, it ceases to be a living Church.

A second thing which the Church has contributed to history is the quality of life by which it is characterized. It manifests love and concern. The Church is no ghetto community, no mutual admiration society, shut up within itself. When it shuts the world out and turns in, it is on the way to death. For it is denying its Lord who went about doing good and caring for the needs of men. It is a striking fact that Jesus began his ministry in Nazareth by reading the prophetic message about clothing the naked, visiting the imprisoned,, feeding the hungry, and preaching the good news to the poor. Furthermore, at the end of his ministry, he related the parable about the Son of Man in the last day. Once more the emphasis falls upon the naked, the hungry, and the imprisoned. It was and is for such men that the Christ gave himself and that he still toils up fresh Calvaries with the Cross upon his back. For his Church, the challenge comes to do likewise, to make up what is lacking in his sufferings.

Across history, the Church has shown its earthiness. Corruption, pride, even sensuality have marred its witness. For it is in the world as well as in the Spirit, and the battle with its creatureliness is always present. Yet the Church has initiated measures of social concern which ultimately have been taken over by the secular order. We think of educational institutions, of hospitals, of institutions for the insane, of homes for orphans and the aged, of concern for the poor and the hungry. Much of the humanitarian concern that characterizes our Western democracies has its roots in the Church. What the Church has initiated, the state has taken over. And significantly, when the Church moves into missionary activity overseas, it continues to build hospitals, to send doctors, to provide colleges and schools, to train in agriculture. Here is a dynamic way in which the Incarnate Eschaton carries on his Christianizing task through his body, the Church.

In our preaching we need to make our people aware of social concerns and to encourage them to support humanitarian projects. Indeed, this is a very real element in the prophetic dimension of preaching. But it also involves giving our hearers a vision of the Christian lifestyle. They need to understand the meaning of Christian love and to be encouraged to cultivate such a spiritual gift in their own lives. The Church must proclaim the Gospel to sinners, but it must also build up its own members in both the understanding and the practice of the Christian faith. In the prayer of General Thanksgiving there is a meaningful phrase which we preachers need to remember. "That we may show forth thy praise, not only with our lips, but in our lives, by giving up ourselves to Thy service and by walking before Thee in holiness and righteousness all our days." There is another familiar phrase in the Church's prayers: "Grant that what we confess with our lips, we may believe in our hearts, and practice in our lives." The building up of the saints in the way of love and service should be a continual challenge from the pulpit.

This brings us to a third aspect of the Church's function in history. The Church is the conscience of the community. Society has no conscience unless some group within it functions in this capacity. The anonymous author of the early Christian tract *Ad Diognetum* stated that what the soul is to the body, the Christian is to the world. The Church is set continually to challenge the conscience of nation, state and society, and this requires prophetic preaching. To this we must turn in the next chapter.

We may close this chapter by reminding ourselves that the Church is not the sole medium of the divine activity in history. It is the special instrument for announcing that redeeming grace which was brought to an effective focus in the Christ-event. But the Christ, Risen and Cosmic, in his transcendent presence, is also immanent and active in his world. Wherever men catch a vision for alleviating human misery and meeting human need, he is there. Even though, like Cyrus the Persian in Deutero-Isaiah (45:4ff), they do not know God, he still works through them. Indeed, often it has been humanists who have manifested "Christian" concern, when the church has been silent! Yet we need to add that such concern often has its source in Christian values which have been secularized in the process of history, so that, in a very real sense, our world is being Christianized and humanized in spite of itself. Sin remains sin, but alienated man manifests an attitude to life and human need which is only possible because the Christ-event has occurred.

Again, we cannot deny all revelation to other religions, even though we believe the disclosure in the Christ-event to be final. There are visions of God, understandings of saving incarnations or avatars, emphases on salvation by faith alone and not by works, which touch the fringes of the Christian revelation. Hinduism and Buddhism reflect insights that point to the Christ as if he has been acting and speaking in their grasping for truth and through their broken visions. When Sadhu Sundar Singh, the converted Hindu mystic, was asked what he found in Christianity that he did not have in Hinduism, his answer was "Jesus Christ." Ramanu-ja believed in a God of love. Buddhist Yodoism is a religion of grace. Only Christianity can really and authentically point to the historicity of God. Yet these other glimpses point to the Christ who pursues all men down through the years, the more so since the Resurrection.

In Masefield's play, *The Trial of Jesus*, Longinus, the Roman Centurian, who stood at the foot of the Cross, is heard talking with Pilate's wife, Procula, just after the Crucifixion. "Do you think he is dead?" she asks him.

"No, lady, I don't."

"Then, where is he?"

"Let loose in the world, lady," replies Longinus, "where neither

Roman nor Jew can stop his truth."

For he is the Alpha and the Omega, the first and the last, and in the end all history will be gathered, judged and redeemed, around him.

4

The Preacher's Prophetic Task
Dealing Hopefully with Principalities and Powers

The biblical witnesses were quite clear that there was a demonic background to human sinfulness and that such demonic forces were operative in the social and political structures of their day. It is true that today we would understand such demonic forces in a different way from the New Testament writers. They were reflecting the cultural outlook of their day and, as we have already emphasized, we cannot absolutize their culture. But we can and must absolutize the revelational insight that the Christ has dealt with the demonic forces in his Cross and Resurrection, and that the powers of this world have already suffered their decisive defeat. Despite the rash of new interest in black magic, in demon possession even to the point of films and novels like *The Exorcist*, and in esoteric speculation, there would seem to be a much more satisfactory understanding, satisfactory in the sense that it does not require credulity while facing squarely the mystery of evil.

We have already dealt with this mystery in large measure, but it is good that we should look into it more deeply, especially at the level of the misuse of human freedom. It is at this level that much of the demonic takes its rise. Modern psychiatry is making us very aware of the psychic forces which are present below the level of human consciousness and of the interplay between them and man's conscious decisions. In addition, modern sociology and group psychology have made us aware of the subterranean forces which become effective in a group. Once a group has surrendered to a certain idea, that idea can become dynamic and take possession of the group. One result is that individual conscience is often suppressed and people perform acts in the mass, in corporate solidarity, that individually they would never accede to. We talk about mass hysteria, about group dynamics, and much of such talk is a modern way of referring to the demonic. Le Bon has said that civilized man descends several steps of the ladder of civilization when he merges himself with the mass. Anonymity becomes a good cover for acquiescing to evil ideas and acquisitive urges which individually we should shun in the broad searchlight of open activity. Thereby we acquiesce in forces which can become demonic. Political, economic and social relationships are in this way shot through with demonic forces which hold man in thrall at all levels of his common life. Our life together is permeated with corruption, and it is so because we ourselves are corrupted. In the end the demonic flourishes because the individual human heart is "exceeding sinful."

If, in our human frailty, we seek to go deeper, we might well trace the mystery back to the two roots—one is the mysterious gift of human freedom, and the other is the element of contingency and chaos present in the creative initiation of this world process. While our human freedom serves to augment and create many of the forces and urges arising in the human unconscious (through the mysterious transmission by genetic heritage), the potential of such forces lies in the depths of our animal ancestry. The roots of the demonic lie in the chaos, contingency and randomness present from the beginning of the process and are especially evident with the emergence of life and the development of consciousness. Without falling into dualism like Edwin Lewis or into a kind of theological schizophrenia like Paul Tillich, we can see the mysterious presence of the chaotic, formless abyss and the consequent unfinishedness without which process and ultimately genuine human freedom could not have been accomplished. As we have seen, the creation and permission of this dimension in the creative process are part of the Cross borne by the Creator.

Now the preacher cannot ignore this demonic element. His hearers are subjected to its presence in their everyday decisions. In their work-a-day life, in the traffic of the market place, in their political decisions and allegiances, in their social relationships—it meets them. And its presence is subtly there in the secret places of their own hearts. Like the apostle Paul, we have to confess that we do not have to wrestle merely with flesh and blood, but with principalities and powers, with spiritual rulers of darkness in high places. The Old Testament prophets had to do just this, and so must the modern preacher. He cannot speak smooth things and proclaim peace when there is no peace. Yet although judgment must be there, there is always the promise of the Gospel, the reinforcing presence of the Christ, and the assurance of his ultimate triumph. Always the prophetic element has this future dimension. It holds the present in tension with that Day when God's purpose will be consummated.

The Dialogue with Civil Religion and the Cultural Capitivity of the Church

Despite our secularity, we Americans have a strange underground of religiosity. Vague and amorphous, it has found frequent expression in our public pronouncements. We pledge allegiance in our clubs and oaths of office to the republic which is "one nation *under God.*" In the Declaration of Independence, we are reminded of the overruling *Divine Providence* and of the laws of nature and *nature's God.* We declare that all men have been endowed by their *Creator* with the inalienable rights of life, liberty and the pursuit of happiness. In his remarkable Gettysburg Address, Abraham Lincoln gave utterance to the hope that "this nation, *under God,* shall have a new birth of freedom." John Kennedy, in his 1961 inaugural address, could state that he had "sworn before you (the nation) and *Almighty God* the same solemn oath our forebears prescribed nearly a century and three quarters ago," and could declare his "belief that the rights of man came not from the generosity of the state but *from the hand of God.*"

Deep down, then, in our American way of life is a kind of civil religiosity. It has its myths and its prophets, its shrines and its martyrs. We go to Washington and see the Washington memorial pointing like a finger up to heaven. We visit the shrine of the prophet and lawmaker, Thomas Jefferson, the American Moses. We go to the shrine of our martyr, Abraham Lincoln, and to the grave of another, John Kennedy. Always there is a kind of religiosity in the background, a kind of belief that we are the chosen of God and have a mission to perform in the world.

"God and freedom" is a cry and a creed. But, at that moment, it is faltering and dying.

The preacher's attitude towards this civil religion tends to be ambivalent. On the one hand, he is bound to welcome any manifestation of religious interest on the part of secular man and secular society. He must also recognize that, however distorted such civil religion may be, its roots lie back in the Christian traditions of the early settlers, especially of the pilgrims of New England. On the other hand, he must recognize the perversion of man's religiosity present in this secularized religion; the completely false understanding of God from the standpoint of the Christian faith; the support which men find in such religion for national arrogance, exploitation of minority groups and small nations, messianic visions of greatness and justification of highly questionable policies.

There is nothing new about all this. Amos had to face in his day the false belief that God was bound to be on Israel's side and that the future was assured despite the social corruption and national wrongdoing. He had to declare a message of doom against a false religiosity. The Day of Yahweh would be darkness and not light. Jeremiah found the people of Judah beset by a false trust in the Temple. Since God dwelt in the holy place, in the sanctuary on Zion's hill, Jerusalem and its people would be secure. No foreign invader could destroy the city, and Judah would survive, be its sin ever so manifestly rampant. Once again the prophetic voice was lifted against a civil religion which ignored the moral bond established in God's covenant with his people. Exile was certain and judgment would fall (Jeremiah 7, 26).

Our civil religion is far removed from its origins in the Plymouth Pilgrims. They interpreted their coming to America on the basis of their Calvinism. They had been brought to the promised land by the exodus through the Atlantic waters. They were the new people of God, and the reign of the saints would be inaugurated. There is considerable evidence that they were postmillenialists. The millenium would occur before the final consummation, but it would inaugurate the End. In it, Christ would reign, but not in Person; he would exercise his power through his saints. The Puritans found it easy to identify their worldly hopes with this millenial expectation. They were to build their "Paradise" in the American wilderness. Their hopes for the future in the new land were expressed in biblical language. Their cry for freedom was mainly concerned with freedom from oppression and with freedom of worship. The latter, however, was interpreted in Calvinistic terms, and thus Baptists, Quakers and others were excluded from the commonwealth. Furthermore, those with no evangelical experience, as Calvinism understood it, had no citizenship. So it was a cry for freedom with all these limitations.

The Pilgrims no longer had to battle with the Roman Church, the scarlet woman, the great whore of Babylon. So they identified the Anti-Christ of their apocalyptic outlook with the Indians and thus sanctified the slaughter and exploitation of their Indian neighbors.

From such roots, civil religion developed. It retained many of the emphases of its origin, but its understanding of God moved further and further from the Christian disclosure. As scientific influences began to be felt and the atmosphere of the European Enlightenment began to be breathed, deism took over from theism, and the emphasis fell upon a transcendent deity who ruled his world by law—natural law and moral law. The thought of grace receded into the background, but the idea of election remained. So also did the idea of freedom, much enlarged in the minds of men like Franklin and Jefferson but still with concern for freedom from oppression. America was elected to become a nation of free men, and it would preach democracy to the world. So the founding Fathers read deism and human freedom into their civil religion. Now every man should worship as his conscience dictated. Now every man had a right to be free, on paper. The Declaration of Independence became the credo for the secular or civil religion which now began to find its place in American life.

The anti-Christ idea remained. It was identified with the British, then with the South in the war between the states, then with Germany, then with Hitler and the Japanese. Every war became a crusade for freedom. The world must be made safe for democracy. Immigrants came to America as to the land of freedom. The task of extending the reign of freedom across the vast land mass of America underlay the economic and property urges which drove the people West. The Anti-Christ was identified with the enemies of the frontier, and the Red Indian tribes paid the price. America denied them freedom in the name of freedom—an irony of history. Civil religion, with all its boasted emphasis on freedom, deprived others of freedom in order to establish its own. Andrew Jackson's treatment of the Cherokees is a living reminder of this.

Complex economic issues as well as the evil of slavery lay behind the grim conflict of the Civil War. There soon developed a religious dimension alongside the political motifs. Lincoln's second inaugural makes it evident: "Yet if God wills that it (the war) continue until all the wealth piled by the bondsman's two hundred and fifty years of unrequited toil shall be sunk, and until every drop drawn with the lash shall be paid by another drawn with the sword, as was said three thousand years ago, so still it must be said, 'The judgments of the Lord are true and righteous altogether.' " The war became one with God on the side of the Union, not the Christian God, but a God of war who was marching on.

Civil religion is mixed up with Christian devotion in Julia Howe's "Battle Hymn of the Republic." An apocalyptic note and a Christian reference are combined with and distorted into a civil religion which sees God on the side of steel and bloodshed, not standing in judgment above it all. The Anti-Christ was slavery and the South! The Christ who was born across the seas stands as an eternal rebuke to slavery and man's exploitation of his brother man. But his God is not to be seen in campfires and arms of war. He is seen, towering above it all, on His eternal cross. The Civil War, and every other war, are the way sinful men destroy themselves and drive God out of his world onto his Cross. This was America's judgment. The South paid and so did the North.

The idea of "Manifest Destiny" continued and carried America across the continent. Then, with no more American frontiers to conquer, imperialistic ambition combined with manifest destiny and its vision of freedom. We went overseas to the Phillippines and the Caribbean. Mark Twain referring to the Philippines, saw the paradox: "I pray you to pause and consider. Against our traditions, we are entering upon an unjust and trivial war, a war against a helpless people, and for a base object— robbery." Today the objective of our exploitation is economic rather than colonial, but the same drive is there. And yet there is a concern to spread freedom. Paradoxically, we possessed the Phillipines and then gave them their freedom in 1934.

This is not Christianity. Periodically it has gained new strength from the Churches. Like a parasite it has benefited by movements like the Great awakening, and yet it has denied the deep evangelical truths for which such movements stand. It still lives on the fringes of our Church life, and often penetrates into the center of that life. For the Church itself is in this world, in the flesh as well as in the Spirit. It is a very human institution, organized and financed like its secular counterparts, and open always to the temptation to increasing secularity. Its allegiance to the

Christ has to be lived out in this world order. It is the ongoing of the Incarnation, but it does not participate in the sinless humanity of its Lord. It is in the process of being redeemed. The principalities and powers that are present in its contemporary culture play upon the lives of its members and inject their false values and distorted religious insights into the very citadel where the Christ continues his conflict with them and their power. For the Church can and often does become a captive to its contemporary culture. What Amos and Jeremiah attacked in the church of ancient Israel has its parallel in our church life today. So often we sell out to our culture. Most of all this is true in the subtle infiltration of civil religious ideas into the thinking and living of the members of the church.

Let us note, first of all, the dangers inherent in civil religion itself. It will not save America despite its belief in America's destiny. Rather, it leads to arrogance. We need as a nation to repent and walk in humility before the living God. but that is not what this vague and amorphous religious consciousness will help us to do. In the nation generally it has slowly become so secularized that any kind of God except America has disappeared. Our people have retained the worship of freedom without the worship of freedom's God. The Kingdom of God has been secularized and identified with America. In the eyes of John Birchers and many other ultra-conservatives, America becomes the world's savior. If there be a God, he is the God of the capitalists, the one who blesses big business, the supporter of conservatism and the deity of the white race! Freedom is no longer freedom under the living God! And, with the kind of God just portrayed, it may cease to be freedom at all! So we find ourselves politically offering freedom and encouraging democracy with one hand, as if we are zealous missionaries for the Statue of Liberty, but with the other hand we expand economic exploitation and seek new markets, including the traffic in armament, with little moral concern or responsibility.

Because civil religion manifests such distortions, it is really no ally to the Gospel. Often man's religious consciousness, where it is authentic, provides a bridgehead where we can point beyond its limited awareness of the divine to the final revelation in the Christ. But this vague civil religiosity is no such help. Rather it is a demonized version of the religious consciousness and can enter into our Church life and vitiate the message of the Christ-event. It appeals to Church people because it is a debased and secularized version of the Christian understanding of God and his world.

It provides some folk with a kind of umbrella under which they can hide from the Gospel and still believe that they are Christian. It is near enough to Christianity to prove attractive to the conservative mind, which desires to preserve the *status quo* in religion and politics. Its tendency to emphasize "having" and to exalt the acquisitive dimension of the American lifestyle appeals to those who want to preserve their pride in their own achievements, not to indulge in too much self-sacrifice, and to retain enough of the "old Adam" to justify a belief in works. Works and not grace is a good way out for the man who wants to be religious at a minimum cost. Furthermore, the nationalistic approach of civil religiosity appeals to a certain type of patriotism. Its whole tendency is away from glorifying the Christian God to glorifying a god dressed in American garb, away from grace to works, away from self-sacrifice and self-giving to acquisition and possession, away from being to having, away from the need for divine forgiveness and human repentance to national arrogance. All this is hardly surprising, for civil religion is the work of sinful man.

No Christian pulpit can leave this issue undealt with. The preacher has to attack civil religion within the church itself, for the church members themselves are often in cultural captivity to their secular environment. They are so conditioned by the cultural atmosphere in which they live that they interpret his sermons in terms of it. They hear what their cultural captivity will let them hear. Their hearing and their thinking are distorted by a framework derived from the vague and amorphous permeating religiosity with its accompanying values. Like a penumbra, this atmosphere hangs on the fringe of and penetrates into our church life. In the South it is blended with Southern culture and still helps to sanctify racism in many Southern minds. In suburbia it is intermixed with suburban mores, with the search for status and the country-club mentality. Everywhere it lifts its head, and the preacher has himself to beware that it does not color his own understanding of the Gospel of grace and distort his message.

When a country has no state-established religion, it proceeds to create one that is far more unchristian than the versions of Christianity which are state established. Thomas Jefferson failed to see this possibility.

The Searchlight on Social Morality and Political Structures

Because the Church is in the world and has a faith which affirms the world, the preacher must address the social and political atmosphere in which his members live their lives. This atmosphere includes the personal values, economic structures, and political relationships in which they are involved. If Christ's redemption promises liberation from sin and every form of oppression, then the prophetic voice must be lifted against every form of exploitation and enslavement which threatens those personal values that center in our freedom as children of God. The pulpit is called upon in every age to diagnose the state of society and offer the remedy in Jesus Christ. The Word of God in the Christ-event cuts across our human systems and worldly values, stripping away our apparent motives and revealing the true state of our hearts. In pronouncing the divine judgment on the world, the preacher must also place the plumbline against the church, for the "saints" are also in the secular society. As we have just seen, the Church always faces the danger of bending the divine will to the human, of glorifying and assuring success to the popular motives and idealisms of the day.

At the center of our human relationships there is the idea of justice. Quite apart from the Christian understanding of man, human historical development has manifested certain natural orders within which patterns of human relationship have been established. These are at the levels of sex, family, economics, race, and community. The last of these five can be divided into various patterns depending upon the extent of the community and its position in the hierarchy of communities. So we have patterns from the local community through the state or national community to the international community. In all of these the concept of justice has its place, but so also has the presence and abuse of power. Indeed, the preacher has to support justice and the presence of the power by which its enforcement is possible, yet he also must attack every abuse of power and every act of injustice which it makes possible.

In the center of the preacher's understanding lies man's sin and the reality of the demonic, for, as we have seen, the demonic becomes more evident and intensified as we move into patterned relationships. Wherever men enter into relationship, the power issue arises. Man in God's image, man as he ought to be, is the man for others, man activated by love and giving himself in the service of God and his fellows. But as Nietzsche said, "There has been only one Christian in the world, and he was crucified on Calvary." Historical man does not manifest such openness to God or to his fellows. He is essentially a morally responsible being, but he has chosen to ignore such responsibility. His love for God and for his fellows is replaced by love for himself. He chooses to be possessive and acquisitive, not self-giving and loving. From looking upwards to God and outwards to his fellows, he chooses to look within. As Reinhold Niebuhr put it, he is guilty of "God-almightiness."

Power becomes thereby perverted and misdirected. We do, however, need to define what we mean, for, in the popular usage, power is thought of in physical terms. It is the physical instrument which is central. We, however, are more concerned with power in its spiritual roots, for the physical aspect of power cannot finally be separated from the intention which guides its use. Power ultimately resides in its spiritual source, in the human or the divine will that directs its physical dimension. King Alfred, the early English King, is reported to have said: "Power is never a good unless he be good that has it." Now, in this sense, the Christ-event discloses that the power of God is the power of self-giving love. Ideally the root of man's power lies in a will that is motivated by love for God and for others. In actuality, the human will be so misdirected that man's power becomes selfish and acquisitive, and physical power is used to fulfill man's selfish and arrogant intentions.

It is just here that the preacher's concern for justice arises. Although his major concern is to evoke love and thus create a community where power is rightly directed, he has to deal with a secular order where personal and social power are abused. Justice, in the time-honored definition, consists in rendering to every man his due. This is to say that every man is an object of duty; he must be treated responsibly, for, in Kant's words, he is an end in himself. This is consistent with the Christian emphasis on the value of the individual under God, and it is the root understanding of justice in our Western democracies. For Christians, such justice is rooted in love, in concern for all men as made in God's image. A just society must preserve the inalienable rights of its citizens and impose by law certain correlative responsibilities. It is concerned to protect personal freedom, but also to safeguard against its perversion to license. Justice is directed towards preserving individual rights and imposing responsibilities if these are not voluntarily accepted. Such imposition and enforcement are necessary even in democracies, because every democracy is a community of sinful men, subject to the abuse of power and the exploitation of persons. So far as is possible, the State exists to exercise its authority, its power, in the service of justice.

Justice is grounded in love, for man can only be treated as an end in himself when he is regarded as of eternal value. The principle of justice in itself contains no appeal to love. But if man is not to be treated as a means to an end, there is the implication that he is fitted for some kind of eternal life. The Christian disclosure makes explicit what is implicit in the idea of justice, and the Christian preacher should emphasize this. Because sinful man will not recognize his responsibilities to his fellow man, justice employs power or authority to enforce such recognition. In a secular and acquisitive society, where love rarely operates, justice by taxation and law enforcement compels a citizen to accept his responsibilities. If he will not voluntarily care for the poor and the indigent, then he is taxed in order to make such care possible. If he is not concerned for the exploited then he must pay for the law to enforce justice in this area. Where love does not operate because of sin, justice by its use of power creates a patterned society where some degree of order is maintained.

Of course, sometimes justice can even operate to see that love is not exercised irresponsibly. There is a story of an Indian Christian who was heavily in debt. He received a large legacy unexpectedly and immediately distributed it to the poor of his neighborhood. He kept none for himself, but he also ignored his large creditors. Christian love can operate freely only when legal obligations have been met. Thus justice ensures and safeguards those human values for which the Christian emphasis on love stands, but it also directs the right exercise of even that love in the ordered relationships of life.

We may express this by saying that whereas Christian love is directive, justice is regulative. Now the preacher must recognize this. He attacks injustice, exploitation, oppression, inequity, lack of responsibility in the name of Christian love. But he must also recognize that, in a secular order, such love must seek for channels of operation and find secularized expression in the judicial and political structures of society. Where such structures fail to offer such expression the prophetic voice must be raised.

Two areas where the preacher tends to be silent are those of economic and political power. Let us look at the issue of economic power. The growth of vast corporations and conglomerates such as the oil corporations has threatened the true exercise of justice. For class interest often overrides competition between such groups. They are concerned to keep up profits, to exploit labor and to rob the public. The news media are often dominated by them, and so also are governments. Bribery cases, now being exposed, offer evidence of this. Over against this and originating in the atmosphere which it creates we have the economic power of the labor unions. The whole situation creates an atmosphere of fear in which preachers, teachers, workers and policiticans are afraid to speak their mind for fear of losing a source of income, losing their job, or losing a position of influence. The economic power thus becomes demonic.

Yet only the Church can raise its voice effectively against exploitation and oppression. It offers a liberating gospel which is concerned with every form of tyranny, every demonry which may rob man of his freedom and treat him as a means to its ends. Excessive profits at the expense of the public, exploitation of workers, bribery in the courts of justice and the halls of Congress, muzzling of the press—all these are the concern of the Church. The Christ-event is concerned with this sinful order.

Take political power. The abuse of such power was very evident in the Nixon years, and we are never completely free of it. Once again the Church cannot be silent. This does not mean that the pulpit should become a political hustings or that the preacher should advocate party partisanship, but it does mean that the Christian congregation should have the Christian searchlight directed upon political policies and their implications, whatever be their party advocacy. Where a policy furthers justice for the individual and delimits the possibility of exploitation, the Church must speak in support. Immediately we think of the high cost of medical care and the need for government control. In a world where medicine increasingly has become a government concern, we in the United States are dragging our feet. Medical men in our congregations may often be a deterrent, but we preachers see our own people suffering from the injustice and exploitation involved, and there comes a time when we must speak in favor of more just enactments. Our Lord made it clear at Nazareth that the healing of the sick and the preaching of the Gospel to the poor and exploited are tasks of the Kingdom. The poor? Yes, and the aged! Once again, justice requires that the Social Security system and its accompanying Medicare be freed of inequities and demonic perversions and that better provisions be made for the aged.

So often the Church has to undertake such work itself and witness in a practical way to its Christian concern. Many state institutions, such as hospitals, institutions for the insane and homes for the aged are secularized versions of Christian experiments. What begins in Christian love and compassion triggers a secular expression and is recognized within the framework of social justice. We have seen this happen in the case of the recognition of the black minority, although here, as so often, much of the Church dragged its legs, and it was humanistic support which made up for the deficiency. (But then our Western humanism has its roots in Christian humanism and lives to some extent as a parasite upon the Christian trunk.)

This is a reminder that the fear of economic and political power can become a demonic tyranny which is evidenced in the cultural captivity of the Church itself. A church which only speaks what the public wants to hear sooner or later ceases to be of use to the public. But so often this is what the Church expects of us preachers. The social implications of the Gospel and its judgment upon the contemporary scene must be replaced by a sentimental Gospel which places no burden upon the consciences of the hearers. You may remember the story of the millionaire at the garden party who is reported to have said: "I can't share my wealth with you; but thank God I can share my Christian faith." The preacher has to point men to the fact that the divine order in the universe is being violated by human sin and demonized power. In so doing, he will not align himself with any political party or any group of economic planners. He will not speak as an idealist or offer a human panacea. In a democracy, he will not identify democracy with Christianity, nor will he regard democratic ways of life as social and political expressions of the Kingdom of God, for he will be aware of the insidious dangers of civil religion. He will not offer a mere diagnosis with a blueprint of social reformation and economic renewal.

Paradoxically, he will recognize the good in such schemes, but like the Irishman who was asked the way to Ballymena, he will say: "Shure, if I was goin' to Ballymena, I wouldn't start from here." For the Christian preacher knows that the world's best is never good enough, that no fine words about equality and freedom can ever be realized without selfishness and greed perverting their realization. He will call men to repentance because, when their best is done, they will still fall short of the City of God. Only God can finally redeem. Even the deist Benjamin Franklin saw this. Recall his prophetic words before our Constitutional Convention two hundred years ago: "I have lived, sir, a long time, and the longer I live, the more convincing proofs I have of this truth, that *God governs in the affairs of men.* And if a sparrow cannot fall to the ground without his notice, is it probable that an empire can rise without his aid? We have been assured, Sir, in the Sacred Writings that 'except the Lord build the house, they labor in vain that build it.' I firmly believe this; and I also believe that, without his concurring aid, we shall suceed in this political building no better than the builders of Babel" ("Motion for Prayers in the Constitutional Convention," *The Most Amazing American: Benjamin Franklin* [Waukesha WI: Country Beautiful, 1973], p. 130).

The preacher will speak as one who has eyes upon God's redemptive act in the Cross and who knows that the claims of the Crucified cover the whole of our corporate as well as our individual life. Here is the remedy for the evils which destroy human society and human personality. Without such redemption, human efforts ultimately fail, and only social action centering in such a Gospel can be finally effective. Thus the preacher speaks always as a man of hope. He points always beyond our creaturely time to God's Time, the end of all history. He knows that this final consummation is already assured by the Resurrection, where our Lord triumphed decisively over our demonries and our sin. Yet, until the Eschaton, we must play our part in fighting evil and supporting the operation of justice. We must be instruments of Christ's Love.

Thus, the preacher seeks to support, actualize and augment schemes of justice, but ultimately he falls back upon the Gospel of grace. Yet here the Church stands condemned. The preacher cannot offer brotherhood to the world when so often the Church has dissolved into blitherhood. Christ has to create fellow ship in the Church first, before the Church can speak of jsutice, let alone love, to the secular order. Yet in the Christ-event there is hope, for he is the incarnate Eschaton, the promise of God's future.

> What can we do, o'er whom the unbeholden
> Hangs like a night with which we cannot cope?
> What, but look sunward, and with faces golden,
> Speak to each other, softly, of a hope
> (F.W.H. Myers, *St. Paul* [London: H.R. Allenson, LTD., no date], p. 34).

The Technological Rape of Nature and the Biological Threat to Personal Being

The Christ-event affirms the world, both human society and the realm of nature. It affirms that the Christ is the Lord of nature as well as of history. The nature miracles recorded in the Gospels point to this, and the New Testament witnesses remind us that the natural order will also be involved in the final consummation. As we have seen, the Cosmic Christ provides the backdrop for that Christ-event which is also the incarnation of the Eschaton. But if the realm of nature also shares in the redemptive event, then the current ecological crisis must figure in the preacher's message. Man was created with scientific and technological gifts. He was made with a capacity to understand the mind of the Creator and thereby to be a responsible steward of the natural. In this unfinished universe he may act creatively and cooperate with the creator in making possible the ultimate consummation. God has put all things under man's feet (Psalm 8), but man in his arrogance and sinful irresponsibility has increased the chaotic aspect of his world rather than shaping and directing it. We do not see all things put under man's feet. But we see Jesus (Hebrew 2:5-9). It is almost as if the author of Hebrews is pointing us to the Christ-event as the key to our contemporary dilemma. Conservation and respect for nature center in the redemptive dynamic which issues from the Cross and Resurrection and moves within the life of the redeemed community.

The Christian preacher must condemn every exploitation of our natural environment, encourage every attempt to conserve and protect it, support every attempt to limit those who are bent on the rape of nature for their own profit, and help Christian people to become aware of their ethical responsibility to the natural order. The prophetic voice needs to be raised against all attempts to pollute our air, poison our streams, destroy our wildlife, turn fertile land into desert and wilderness. In other words, we preachers have to attack the irresponsible technological rape of nature in the interest of material gain and other human pleasure, as in safaris. We turn our lakes into chemical tanks, contaminate our water tables, denude the earth of vegetation and thereby upset the balance of oxygen and carbon dioxide in our atmosphere, and pour our poisonous wastes and ill-conceived insecticides into our rivers, ultimately bringing about the death of our oceans. All in the interests of greed and selfish exploitation! Our continuing destruction of the fine balance of nature, our upsetting of the air and water cycles by pollution, our poisoning of fish and wildlife by industrial waste poured into our waters, our undermining of the ecological pyramid with its balanced structure of food supply—all these are coming home to us in judgment. In destroying nature, we are bringing about our own destruction. When the Old Testament writers saw that man's sin brings back the primordial chaos and turns the garden into a desert, they were pointing out a truth which today is being actualized. Man and his natural environment are bound together by the will of the Creator. When man fails to accept his moral responsibility towards nature, in the end he destroys himself.

Now this means that prophetic preaching needs to remind people of a dimension of moral responsbility which has been strangely ignored in the Christian Church. If we treat our fellows as "Its," as means to our ends, it is even easier to treat nature as an "it" to be used for the technological enrichment of the human species. It is so difficult to envisage nature in other than physical terms even though, at the biological level, its vital dimension is so evident. But that it is capable of psychic response and, at its own level, can demand responsible treatment and behavior on our part—this insight demands a view of nature different from that which the objectivizing and analytical methods of science afford.

Martin Buber has emphasized this kind of distinction by distinguishing the "I-It" and "I-Thou" types of relationships. The scientific and technological approach is characterized by the former. Mechanical causation holds an unlimited reign in the world of It, and this is "of fundamental importance for the scientific ordering of nature" (Martin Buber, *I and Thou*, trans. Gregor Smith [Edinburgh: T. & T. Clark, 1937], p. 51). But man, in his freedom, is not limited by the world of It. He can continually leave it for the I-Thou relation. Indeed, although his characteristic attitude to a tree will be that of I-It, he may yet move into an I-Thou relation with it, a mutual relation of responsiveness, aware that there is a depth here which the scientific attitude cannot disclose (ibid,, pp. 74). Buber contends that the I-Thou relationship with nature is not only possible but may also yield a rich harvest of understanding.

Karl Heim and A. N. Whitehead, each in his own way and from different philosophical approaches, have echoed this viewpoint. Like Buber, they point out that the process of objectification is associated with a time lag, so that the objectified world of "It" is always a past world, a world that has already become. Whitehead speaks of objectification as occurring when an actual entity has attained satisfaction, already attained its goal. He and Heim see the present as a realm of dynamic activity and relationship. Heim points to energy and life as belonging, along with the self-transcendent I of personal being, to the non-objectifiable realm of the dynamic present. We cannot objectify them, but only what they do (Karl Heim, *God Transcendent*, trans. E. Dickie [London: Nisbet, 1953], pp. 132ff.). His whole argument points to a psychic aspect of nature, even at the physical level, akin to will and spirit. The present is "the space of the non-objectifiable, of those possibilities, potencies, powers and volitions, which have not yet become actual" (ibid., p. 136).

Whitehead and his followers likewise offer a view of the world in panpsychic terms and regard it as bound together by feeling. This feeling finds its supreme expression in love, and is brought to a focal point in the love of God. Whitehead contended that science was guilty of "the fallacy of misplaced concreteness." By this he meant, among other things, the mechanistic and causative view of nature. He was attacking the method of carving nature up into solid lumps of matter, separated in space and time and related by a structure of mechanical causation. From such a world any idea of sensitivity is excluded. Whitehead contended that the basic model for nature should be organic. Nature was intimately related internally. Each natural entity was related to all others by a sensitivity which Whitehead described as "prehension." This is a rudimentary feeling for other entities. At higher levels of complexity, it attains conscious feeling and personal apprehension. Thus Whitehead and his followers see the whole universe as knit together by a structure of feeling at various levels of unconsciousness and consciousness. They have developed a panypsychic view of the universe, seeing nature as shot through with psychic response. Hartshorne and others find the key model for this in human love and see the whole universe under the persuasion of divine love (see especially C. Hartshorne, *Reality as a Social Process* [Boston: Beacon Press, 1953]; Daniel Day Williams, *The Spirit and the Forms of Love* [New York: Harper & Row, 1968]; N. Pittenger, *Process Thought and Christian Faith* [New York: The Macmillan Co., 1968]).

All this underlines the fact of scientific abstraction. Nature is no closed box dominated by mechanical causation. We do not have to accept any of the philosophical structures to which we have referred, but we do need to listen to this attack upon our science-dominated viewpoint and to pay heed to its insights into the psychic dimension of nature. There is an I-Thou relationship to nature which we ignore at peril. When we look deeper than the scientific abstraction can take us, we recognize that nature too may be capable of psychic response at all levels. T. E. Jessup of the University of Hull reminds us that nature "is a closed system only as presented by the sciences, which on principle, for the sake of intellectual tidiness, ignore man's action in it and on it, and thereby turn it into an abstraction, a neat fiction, a logical whole but an unreality" (T. E. Jessup,

Science and the Spiritual, [London: Sheldon Press, 1942], p. 61).

So we can listen to Albert Schweitzer, controversial figure though he was. He made the main premise of his philosophical stance, a "reverence for life." He noted the tendency of Western and Oriental philosophers alike to limit ethical concern to the human level. For him all things were activated by a will to live, and thus there must be a reverence for even cells and crystals (Albert Schweitzer, *Civilization and Ethics*, trans. C. T. Campion [London: A. & C. Black, 1945], p. 213). He recognized the dilemma presented by the ecological pyramid, namely, the way in which life lives on life in order to preserve the ecological balance. He wrote: "Again and again we see ourselves under the necessity of saving one living creature by destroying or damaging another" (A. Schweitzer, *Indian Thought and Its Development*, trans. Mrs. Charles E. Russell [Magnolia Mass: Peter Smith, 1962], p. 84). Indeed, so extreme was his position that he sadly reflected that to cure sleeping sickness involves the killing of the disease-causing germs. Instead of recognizing the chaotic aspect of nature, he thus ventured on the sentimental. He did, however, counsel an ethical reverence for the ecological pyramid which endeavors to prevent its excesses: "So far as he is a free man he (man) uses every opportunity of tasting the blessedness of being able to assist life and avert from it suffering and destruction" (Albert Schweitzer, *Out of My Life and Thought*, [London: George Allen & Unwin, 1933], p. 272). His final comment on traditional Christianity is significant: "Even when sympathy with the animal creation was felt to be right, it could not be brought within the scope of ethics, because ethics were really focused only on the behavior of man to man" (ibid., p. 272). Leaving on one side the near pantheism of Schweitzer with his emphasis on the Will-to Live, immanent in all things, he is yet pointing to a vital lack in the Christian understanding of ethical responsibility.

When we face the challenge of such a diverse array of thinkers, we realize that an I-Thou relationship with nature is an essential part of our Christian existence. We need to recognize our oneness with nature and to seek to grasp its spiritual meaning. We who transcend nature as self-conscious spirits are yet also one with nature from which we have emerged by God's creative act. We preachers need to evoke this kind of response. We need to encourage an acceptance of the natural order and its creatures for what they are, a reverence for their particular type of being, a concern for their freedom from suffering and frustration within the limits that the ecological balance permits, a recognition of their kinship with us.

The practical aspect of this recognition of kinship lies in our use of scientific knowledge and technological skill. Prophetic preaching involves an attack on all misuse of such knowledge and skill. It also calls for their use to remove any imbalance of nature, to purify and maintain its cycles, and to remedy its tragedy and suffering. We need to call for the liberation of nature from our arrogant exploitation and from subjugation to our selfish economic ends. We must point to man's position as a steward under God and emphasize his ethical responsibility to the whole of God's creation.

In doing this, the preacher needs to stress the unfinished nature of the universe. We have already referred to this and described man as a co-creator with God. Man's scientific ability is the developmental result of the God-given capacity to be a vicegerent over the created order. The divine injunction to have dominion over the creatures carries with it the obligation to exercise such dominion responsibly. Furthermore, such dominion is directed towards preparing even nature for its perfected participation in the fulfillment of the divine purpose. The Christ-event carries the promise that *all* things will ultimately be summed up in Christ, things in heaven and things on earth. The ultimate destiny of the world is not the *megalopolis* that technocratic man is trying to build. It is *Incarnopolis*. Our hope is that the God who drew history into himself in Jesus will ultimately incarnate himself in the whole process.

So the preacher must keep men's eyes on the future as well as on the present. He must challenge men to live and work within such a tension. The End is God's act, but we cannot lie back and leave it to Him. There is a parody of the well-known hymn "Rise up, O men of God," which points to this dangerous mood.

> Sit down, O men of God,
> His Kingdom He will bring
> When most of all it pleases Him,
> You cannot do a thing.

Moltmann has described our true Christian stance as "creative discipleship." We are called to play our part in the coming of God's *Eschaton*. In Christ's name we are called to liberate the potencies and powers in man and in our world which make possible the ultimate consummation of God's Kingdom. At the level of nature, we may be instruments of God's creative power as we liberate the warped and bound potencies of our world and restore the structures that men have marred. So we may play our part in hastening God's Day, for to some degree, he waits on us for that final act in which he will fill the universe with his glory, his presence. In calling us to be his co-workers, he has left open, to some degree, the routing and the timing of the fulfillment of his purpose. Yet, in the end, he will win his way and gather the whole process into his life. He suffers, he rejoices, he journeys with us, that we and nature ultimately may be brought to live in that life and become a part of that Incarnapolis which he intends. Prophetic preaching must challenge man to his co-creatorhood with God.

A good setting for such preaching would be celebration and joy in God's creative work. We have so often forgotten that our God rejoiced in his creation and declared it to be good because it contained potentially all the possibilities for the realization of his purpose. So, like the sons of God who shouted with joy on the morn of creation (Job 38:7), we too celebrate the beauty and wonder of the created order. This provides the setting for striving, both to fight the demonic perversions to which technology is subject and to direct nature to the service of God's plan. Francis of Assisi in his great "Canticle of the Sun," could recognize his kinship with all living things. So he could sing of brother sun and sister moon, of brother wind and sister water, of brother fire and mother earth, praising his and their Creator for the role they played in his own life. Against such a backdrop, a prophetic attack and challenge can be driven home.

The concern of the Church with man's scientific developments is not only directed upon the technological rape of nature, but increasingly it must be focused upon the biological investigation of man's genetic structures. We have developed rapidly in the last decades our understanding of the hereditary factors in human personality, and we are learning increasingly how to manipulate them. Such "genetic engineering" can be beneficial, but it can also be a threat to personal values and to the Christian understanding of man. It often raises ethical issues which the Church seems generally to ignore.

Our knowledge has reached the point at which we know the chemical structure of the genetic molecules that carry the hereditary factors of human personality throughout the living cells of the human organism. We have increasing understanding of their coding and of the mechanisms by which they both control the growth of the organism and also determine its physical characteristics and many of its psychological traits. We are beginning to isolate scientifically the coded structures which determine the sex of a human embryo. We are also identifying and learning to isolate the deformations of genetic structures which presage prenatal defects. Before long we shall be so manipulating the female eggs and male sperms of human beings that we can predetermine sex and also remove and replace defective genes which will produce ill effects in the resulting child. By developing vitreous wombs and fertilizing human eggs outside the female womb, we are getting to the stage of substituting a controlled process for the normal way of human procreation.

The preacher needs to address himself to such issues at three levels. Firstly, he must remind his hearers that outright condemnation of such scientific procedures involves a denial of the Christian belief that man is to be a co-creator with God. Man's scientific ability is a divine gift by which he may deal with the unfinished nature of this universe and cooperate with his Creator in completing the process. One major problem that man faces is the presence of evil in his world, a demonic twist which has polluted the gene pool and introduced suffering and deformity into the womb and beyond. The preacher should welcome any scientific process by which such demonic distortions can be dealt with and prenatal defects corrected. Here scientific advances have much to offer.

Secondly, however, the preacher must decide how far the artificial production of human embryos contravenes the natural processes ordained by the Creator and what it implies for the Christian understanding of procreation. If Christian marriage is sacramental at the level of the physical union, and if Christian love finds sacramental expression at the level of sex, then the Christian conscience must be exercised when artificial fertilization and vitreous wombs are advocated. Aldous Huxley's *Brave New World* becomes a reality, and the process of naturalistic reductionism removes Christian values from the realm of human relationships.

Thirdly, and closely related to this, the preacher must consider how far unnatural development of a human fetus in a vitreous womb rather than a human womb can affect the child so produced. (This has not yet been effected.) We do not know how much the natural environment can affect the human person prenatally. More is involved than heredity in human development, even at the prenatal stage.

Other issues of import for Christian moral understanding keep raising their heads. There is, for instance, the serious problem raised by cloning, already being successfully undertaken experimentally with the lower creatures. Here the nucleus of an ordinary cell of the human body would be inserted into a human egg to replace the nuclear material there present. In this way, it is argued, exact reproductions of the person from whom the nucleus was taken could be produced, to any desired number. Again, environmental influences are ignored at the pre-and post-natal stages, but the issue is a fearsome one and raises real questions for the Christian understanding of personality.

Perhaps more challenging are experiments being undertaken with human genetic material and human fetuses. These reduce man to the animal level and ignore our Christian claim that, though emerging from the evolutionary process, man is distinguished by being created in the image of God. There are issues raised here like those associated with how late in the developmental process abortions may take place. When does the fetus become human and infanticide become a reality?

Enough has been said to remind preachers that the field of their preaching is much wider than they themselves are prepared to admit. If the Church is the conscience of the community, then that conscience is most of all manifested, educated and directed by the Christian pulpit. Woe betide us if we fail at this crucial point!

5

The Preacher's Ultimate Objective
Building Bridges to the Secular Society

In undertaking the communication of the Gospel to the contemporary scene, the preacher has to remember the peculiar atmosphere of the society to which he is called to witness. We have already noticed certain characteristic aspects of the contemporary scene, while also calling attention to those permanent insights in the Christian message by which they are to be interpreted. It is this interplay between the permanent insights of the Gospel and the historically transient aspects of the contemporary culture which presents a basic problem for the preacher. Every age requires its own hermeneutic, for the disclosure in the Christ-event has to be translated into a historical garb appropriate to that age. The basic problem is one of communication. How can the Gospel of grace be made intelligible in the thought forms of an age without the loss of those saving insights which make it effective in men's lives? This ever-recurring problem is peculiarly critical in our own time because of the domination of the scientific approach to reality and its tendency to eclipse all thoughts about the transcendent. We may label our society secular, but we need to remember the peculiar qualities of this secularity.

In the process of human history, the "secular" has described a concern with this temporal order as contrasted with the "sacred," which referred to the eternal or supernatural. In the medieval period, the secular was, however, subordinated to the sacred, and the Holy Roman Emperor was a servant of the Church. The medieval city centered in the Cathedral with its gothic spire pointing like a finger up to heaven. Man was preoccupied with his sins and his eternal destiny. Culture had a religious focal point. Men wrote, sang, carved and painted around the theme of the Christ-event.

With the Reformation and the rise of modern science, the secular and the sacred became increasingly divorced. The secular came to describe the this-worldly concern, the realm of human affairs, and the sacred became the description of man's religious activities. The City of Geneva and the Puritan colonies of New England are lingering traces of the attempt to make the two realms coterminus. By the time of the Enlightenment, however, their divorce became increasingly evident, and man's religious activities began to drop into the background of his social life and cultural values. We describe this by saying that human life became secularized. The increasing success of natural science and its description of the world as subject to unbreakable laws ruled out miracle and revelation. The words of the hymn—"Laws that never shall be broken / For their guidance Thou hast made"—describe the God of the "founding fathers" of our American republic, the God of Thomas Jefferson, John Adams, and Benjamin Franklin. This deity was not the Christian God, but a God majestic in his transcendence, who had created a world governed by natural and moral law. This was a law-regulated universe, a closed box in which God did not intervene. No break such as miracle or revelation could occur in its continuously regulated process of natural cause and effect. We forget that Jefferson's Bible excised all references to miracle and specific saving disclosures. It was the time of Voltaire, Diderot, John Locke, and Tom Paine, the age when Harvard went Unitarian and many Congregational and Baptist churches left the evangelical fold. The secular age was beginning, and it has been with us ever since. Its prophet was August Comte, who envisaged a world completely dominated by scientific methodology, from which all supernatural reference could be banished—whether in the language of religion or in the speculations of metaphysics. The age of scientific positivism had dawned.

Since then, across two hundred years, scientific research and technological achievement have produced a world in which, to a large extent, any thought of God has vanished. The secular has taken over, the sacred has been banished, and the thought of a God who is concerned in our human affairs has been largely eclipsed. In our time, the secular city is characterized by a secularism which regards scientific achievement as central, the forces and processes of nature as all-determining, and the only knowledge that is reliable as that which is related to the this-worldly order. Science, from the physical and biological sciences through the realms of psychology and sociology, has become the sole repository of dependable knowledge. Morality has been reduced to a description of the best kind of behavior for human survival in the conflicting jungle of natural forces. Religion becomes a useful instrument for enabling man to achieve some degree of personal integration in the face of a hostile environment.

The secular has become the realm of human achievement, especially through the use of the scientific ordering of human life and the processes of nature. It is the realm where human thinking and rational endeavor have succeeded in producing a wealth of knowledge which has no reference to God and which seems to be achieved without any supernatural assistance. It has produced secular man, the man who needs no transcendent presence to guide his living, the man who believes his human knowledge sufficient to guide his life, the autonomous man who must decide his existence without God. Intoxicated by its scientific success, such a culture has been characterized until recently by a kind of secular optimism. The control of nature and the scientific organization of society have seemed to give promise of an unlimited future. There is nothing that scientific knowledge and technological skill cannot accomplish to better man's material setting and assure him of a physically secure life. Now this optimism is being challenged, and secular man remains enthroned in a growing uncertainty. To this world the preacher has to build bridges of communication and re-establish a bridgehead for the sacred.

The Eclipse of God and the Lost Sense of Transcendence

One aspect of the preacher's problem is how to convey a sense of transcendence to a world from which thoughts of transcendence have disappeared. We can see this immediately in the way in which areas have been increasingly placed under the aegis of human achievement which were formerly left to the realm of religious concern. Three hundred years ago, when a famine came, men could only pray to God, but now modern

agricultural techniques have succeeded where religion was not too successful. Three hundred years ago, when pestilence and disease struck,
men turned to divine assistance, but now modern medicine and our
wonder drugs have achieved what God did not seem to do very well.
Three hundred years ago, the insane were left to God, often bound in
chains and cabined near the church sanctuary, but now modern psychiatry
has accomplished what religion with all its praying rarely achieved. An
atmosphere has been created where God seems to have been driven out of
the picture, and where man acts as if God were not there. The success of
science and its method has blinded our eyes to the creative Presence.

We have forgotten that science is the child of the Christian faith. It
came to birth when men were led to devise new ways of understanding
the mind of the Creator by the investigation of his creative works. Most
of the early natural scientists were Christian men—take for instance
Galileo, John Newton and John Ray. As we have already seen, science is
God's gift in order that we men may cooperate with our Creator in
completing his creative intention for his world. With increasing control,
however, arrogance has replaced humility before the mystery of creation.
Bronowski's best-seller and television program *The Ascent of Man*, can
describe our scientific achievement without one reference to God. The
two-tier universe has been supplanted by a flat landscape. Heaven and
the supernatural no longer come into man's preview. The sense of the
transcendent has been banished from man's everyday procedures. Many
regard religion and the churches as anachronistic overhangs of past
superstitions.

In meeting this challenge, we do not attack science. Rather we need
to attack the fallacy that science is the only sure and certain way of
knowing. We ourselves, as preachers, need to be aware of its limitations.
But we cannot deny its positive findings and unchallengable successes. It
is not science that we need to attack but the naturalism which springs
from an over-exaggerated faith in scientifical method as the sole repository of knowledge. Such a viewpoint denies all moral and spiritual values
and explains them by reduction to purely naturalistic urges and desires.
They do not offer any insight into reality but are merely illusory con-
structs by which man seeks to survive in a hostile environment. Science
can master that environment and, in the end, abolish such fictitious
appraisals of reality. The transcendent will be abolished and the idea of
God no longer needed.

Such a viewpoint lacks consistency. The sciences upon which it leans involve a quest for truth which basically assumes that the universe is rational. Even the scientist who is naturalistically inclined assumes this. But if he does, he has no right to deny that any other experience may not have its objective counterpart. To accept as true the accumulated knowledge which the scientific refinement of sense experience offers and to deny the objective validity of moral and religious experience is to disclaim the rationality of the universe. If my natural appetites and desires, such as sex and hunger, have the possibility of objective satisfaction, it would be irrational indeed to affirm that our spiritual desires and experiences are illusory. Because no physical satisfaction is offered for such spiritual yearnings, this does not mean that reality does not offer satisfaction. As C. S. Lewis suggests: "A man may love a woman and not win her; but it would be very odd if the phenomenon called "falling in love" occurred in a sexless world" (*The Weight of Glory* [Grand Rapids: Wm. B. Eerdman's 1965], p. 6). If the truth lures us on, then aesthetic, moral and religious valuations cannot be far behind.

We preachers ought to speak more about beauty than we do. It is almost as if we forget the biblical phrase, the "beauty of holiness." Yet the church has, except for Puritan reactionism, always believed that art may portray and point to the heart of reality, that aesthetic value finds its source in God. In man's search for beauty, he finds himself straining against the limits of encompassing transcendence. All our creative efforts at aesthetic expression and our appreciation of beauty point to a harmony in reality which transcends our finite experience. There is an order and harmony behind our world which directly evokes an aesthetic response. Even in science, it is significant how large a part aesthetic evaluation plays in the formulation of satisfactory scientific models. Max Planck speaks of the scientist as sending forth groping feelers of his thoughts in which a vivid intuitive and artistically creative imagination plays its part (*A Scientific Autobiography* [London: Williams and Norgate, 1950], p. 109). We experience harmonious wholeness with immediacy. We do, of course, need that our aesthetic appreciation be educated, but we are aware directly of a given wholeness. Here is a dimension of reality that pervades and yet transcends that physical realm which impinges on our senses and with which science is concerned. We have a feelingful awareness of a patterned harmony which gives us aesthetic pleasure. It is knowledge of the objective, and it is knowledge other than that which science provides.

Beauty does not rest in the eye of the beholder. It is offered to us, waiting to be discovered, and our failure to appreciate it arises out of our defective responses, our lack of education, or our concentration upon the physical to the exclusion of what transcends it and orders it harmoniously. The more we pursue this vision of beauty and harmony, the more it lures us on, until we know that the ultimately beautiful too is part of that transcendent mystery which sets the horizon for our finitude. The great musicians and artists have ever sought to express some vision of that ineffable beauty that lures them on. Without such a vision of transcendence, great art degenerates into technical manipulation of materials. But mere cleverness can never replace the lure of the absolute and the knowledge that it brings. Preaching can help to unveil for people this aspect of reality which our technological and materialistic civilization sadly obscures. It is one way of awakening people to transcendence and of preparing the minds of men for the unveiling of the transcendent mystery in the Christ-event. Here poetic quotations will help.

Again, modern science cannot really evade the objective reality of moral claim, and apologetic preaching needs to bring this to the fore. Science cannot give us ethical direction, and yet the true scientist is still a moral man. He does possess a conscience, a fact very much manifested by the protest registered by a group of scientific researchers against the employment of atomic warfare. The scientist does have an appreciation for human values. Science misdirected may eclipse the divine presence, but it does not obliterate the scientific conscience. Many scientists remain humanists, even when they reject God. Often this moral conscience, which is found in a humanist strain in our culture generally, is exerted because of the spiritual capital stored up by generations of godly forebears. Such humanism plays an important part in the current attempts to establish eco-justice. The finest men of science show a moral concern even when they are not religious. There is a feeling of obligation to pursue the good and to behave rightly. With the eclipse of the transcendent and the supernatural, there is an almost inevitable descent through humanism to naturalism; and, coincidentally, from some concern for moral and human values to permissiveness and the eclipse of man. Yet our culture tends to stay in the moral and humanistic penumbra which surrounds the eclipsed area of transcendence, and never to sell out completely to naturalism.

Here, at least, the preacher has a point of contact. For moral experience points to something objective in the universe. Beneath so much of our moral behavior there is a tacit awareness of some absolute demand, some mysterious depth which underlies our moral compulsion, even at the level of humanism. There is a compulsion of absolute demand in, with and under our relative attempts to express our moral obligation. Peter Burger points to signs of this continuing sense of transcendence in our secular society. He points to the presence of hope as parents reassure their children about the worthwhileness of life in this world; to the reality of human outrage and condemnation of acts of injustice which violate the very nature of man but which seem beyond human rectification and retribution; to courage and hope in the face of death. He sees them not merely as human projections but as reflections of transcendent reality. He argues that what, at the scientific and sociological level, might be described as a human projection may yet in another frame of reference "appear as a reflection of divine realities" (Peter Burger, *A Rumor of Angels* [Garden City: Doubleday Anchor Books, 1970], pp. x, 27). For him they should provide legitimate springboards for launching into a defense of theological transcendence, of the reality of a moral divine presence. They are certainly indications that man cannot escape a tacit awareness of the moral structure which underlies his world, that absolute claim which meets men everywhere, in their personal relations and even in the way in which they direct their scientific discoveries and use their technological skills.

Theodore Roszak has analyzed our cultural crisis by pointing to the way in which the scientific world view has become monolithic and systematically eliminated transcendence. All our transcendent aspirations have been consistently translated into purely secular equivalents. In consequence, men have been confined to an artificial environment in which human values have slowly been lost and morality has been sacrificed to the pursuit of technocratic goals. He writes: "Until we find our way once more to the experience of transcendence. . . there will seem to us no 'realistic' future other than more of the same" [monolithic vision and artificial environment] (T. Roszak, *Where the Wasteland Ends* [Garden City: Doubleday & Co. Inc., 1972], passim). But such an experience is what we preachers have to offer.

Further more, we can hear rumblings which make it clear that all is not well with this flat world, this one-dimensional perspective. A new interest in Zen Buddhism, in esoteric cults, in the use of psychodelic drugs—all manifest this. We dare to believe that the search for transcendence is brought to a focus in the Christ-event. It is significant that Mircea Eliade points in this direction in his own phenomenological investigation of the sacred and the profane. In his examination of primitive religions with their symbols and myths, he finds the fundamental meaning of life, reality, in the awareness of the sacred. In the primordial myths and symbols with their associated rituals, archaic man sought to conform himself to reality and so attain meaning for his existence. The profane or secular found its meaning in the sacred. This occurred in recurring moments when ritual opened a way to sacred space. In this way history took on a circular pattern, always returning to the sacred. But with the process of temporal development, history became desacralized, and the repetitive movements of the cyclic times of the primordial myths were eliminated. History took on a non-repetitive and linear form, and man lost the source of meaning in the return to the sacred. Profane man was driven out from the eternal return of archaic mythology and irremediably identified with history. He can never return to a sacred or transcendent ground uncontaminated by time and becoming (M. Eliade, *Cosmos and History* [New York: Harper Torchbooks, 1959]l, p. 89). For Eliade, the only hope for the recovery of ultimate meaning lies in the Hebrew Christian faith, which takes history seriously and does not try to escape from it as do the cyclic myths and rituals. The Christian faith sees history as a linear movement towards an ultimate consummation. Hence, in this secularized society, in the formation of which the Christian faith has played such a significant role, the Christian understanding of transcendence can still hold the key, provided Christians do not adopt a pied-piper stance!

The Eclipse of Man and the Crisis of Meaning

If science misdirected has led to the eclipse of God, it is also hastening the eclipse of man. When the scientific approach becomes so pregnant that transcendent dimensions of human knowledge are banished, man becomes central and humanism supplants the concern with God. But man, the thinking reed, is dwarfed by the star-spangled depths of infinite space, and his dignity is threatened by the long stream of animal ancestors from which he ultimately evolved. It is one thing to see man, in the light of faith, as loved by a God of the infinite spaces who has himself become man. It is one thing to see the evolutionary development as a creative process directed towards the creation of a being capable of fellowship with his Creator. But it is quite another thing to banish all thoughts of such a transcendent presence, for then man becomes an alien in his world, an accidental by-product of a natural process. He may be arrogant with his scientific knowledge, but sooner or later any meaning for human existence will be called into question. The little waif of the eternities begins to wonder why he is here at all.

This question is faced by the so-called atheistic existentialists. Here we find humanism confronted by the haunting question—"Why am I something and not nothing?" Kierkegaard and Pascal found the meaning of existence in God and his disclosure in the Christ-event. Nietzsche, freed from the idea of the supernatural and transcendent, took refuge in the thought of the superman who can tower above his environment. Even the humanist, with his moral concern, stands alone, beset by nothingness on every side. Camus has explored this in his novels. Jean Paul Sartre has plunged still more deeply into the problem of freedom and what it means to be free, a being whose decision has to be made over an abyss of nothingness.

With the transcendent banished, men put their faith in the empirical realm and the immanent structures of the world. They seek to find the meaning of existence in such structures, and they find that they fail to satisfy. The average person does not indulge in the philosophical excursions of Camus and Sartre, but the same concerns are reflected. In our social structures, naturalism increasingly asserts itself against humanistic moralism; permissiveness raises its head, and a permissive society tends to replace one with an inner core of moral fibre. As society thus becomes more and more naturalized and permissive, people derive their secular goods from the social patterns, economic structures and naturalistic urges of the human situation—family, possessions, work, sex, pleasure. Kierkegaard would have described this as the aesthetic level of existence. He argued that such goods bring men to despair. All of them lack enduring worth and are subject to the process of change which pervades the immanent realm. The breakup of social groupings and the ever-present threat of economic instability have brought crisis to such priorities in our time.

Furthermore, a society based on such priorities begins to disintegrate. Kafka's novel *The Castle* offers a prophetic analysis of our situation. A certain Mr. K. is hired to be bailiff for a group of employers who live in a castle. The latter is situated on a tall mountain and towers above the village beneath. Mr. K. arrives at the village and seeks to communicate with his employers, but all means of communication are blocked. Garbled instructions from his employers somehow reach him, but as he seeks to perform his tasks, he finds that the villagers will not cooperate. His failure to communicate with his employers is thus matched by a break in relationship with the villagers among whom he has to live. The castle may well be a symbol for transcendence. Once relationship to God is cut off, society also falls apart. Man's life loses its basic meaning when he loses contact with the sacred. Faint signals from the castle might at least suggest that there are still faint intimations of transcendence such as we have already seen.

Once man has finally slipped down the inclined plane from humanism to naturalism, he loses what dignity he may possess as a morally responsible and thinking reed. The paradox of being morally responsible, when there is no transcendent ground for such responsibility, disappears completely. Man is now no longer a morally responsible and thinking reed but a reed shaken by the winds of natural urges and energies. Morality is now reduced to a strategy for human survival in the battleground of evolutionary struggle. Thinking becomes nothing creative but a product either of unconscious urges or of cultural conditioning.

Psychology now takes on a naturalistic coloring. We have Freud making man a victim of his unconscious, a mere cork tossed about on various manifestations of his sexual libido. For the advocates of such an understanding of man, man's thinking powers become mere rationalizations of the irrational impulses of his hidden being. Again, we find B. F. Skinner celebrating that man has lost his freedom and dignity. Man becomes a culturally conditioned being. His meanings and values are determined by his immediate cultural environment. He is subjected to a total brainwashing in his Skinnerian social box. Believing that our present culture needs to be changed in order to alter human nature, Skinner advocates change. Since all ideas and meanings are produced by and are reflections of the current culture, it is difficult to see how such a change is possible. Presumably, with all his denial of true selfhood and free creativity, Skinner is the elect one who can transcend the process and provide a new set of meanings for the rest of us. Skinner replaces God. A witty friend of mine once remarked of the agnostic English philosopher C. E. M. Joad: "Dr. Joad believes in God but he pronounces him with a soft G and a long O." Such a view robs man of true selfhood and deprives his existence of any meaning.

To sum up the situation which the preacher faces: Our generation confronts a crisis of meaning. The eclipse of God has brought about the eclipse of man. Once the divine transcendence is ignored, man's own self-transcendence is challenged. Since God no longer enters man's flat landscape, psychological counselling takes the place of spiritual direction. In the secular city, psychiatrists have replaced the preachers. And they are kept busier than ever, for man has lost his raison d'être. His meaning has often turned upon his family and his social structures. But even these immanent groupings are falling apart. Man begins to find that he does not count in our mass economy, so he finds little or no satisfaction in his work. His science and technology give him no enduring vision. The alternatives before him are naturalism or humanism. Either he may identify with the forces that direct the natural process and surrender himself to the sensual, or he may strive valiantly by his own strength of will to build some meaning for his existence in the face of ultimate annihilation and death. Small wonder that alcohol and drugs, sensual enjoyment and violent crime fill the scene, matched by an increasing number of suicides.

Somehow the Christian preacher has to penetrate this situation and affirm man's significance as a personal being. He must point to the basic meaning of human existence as this is lived out in the Christ-event. He has at least a point of contact in that modern man is increasingly aware of his lostness. By this I do not mean "lost" in the Christian sense, but "lost" in the sense of existence being devoid of meaning. Man feels that he is not a whole being. He feels himself alienated from his fellows and his own true self, estranged from meaningful existence, a divided being who cries out for a new unification and wholeness. Everywhere, even in pop music, we hear the cry "who am I?" and "I want to be me." In his secular way, man is asking, "How can I be made whole?" The tragedy is that he turns to the psychiatrist or to the advocate of some esoteric cult rather than to the Christian message. The new interest in transcendental meditation and Zen Buddhism provides yet other ways of transcending the tensions and polarities of human existence. Yet the very use of words like "alienation" and "estrangement" should provide us with a bridgehead for the Christian Gospel of liberation and whole personhood. Man is beginning to realize that enduring meaning, meaning that does not end in frustration, despair or nihilism, needs a transcendent reference. To such a world we come with the Christ-event as a disclosure of meaning and transcendence.

Can we communicate it? Here is the issue, for in a secular society, from which the idea of the transcendent has been eliminated, how does one communicate transcendence? Since all our language is bound to the this-worldly, what is the nature of religious language and how does it communicate what transcends this world? Again, science uses a refined form of language tied to sense experience, and statements in such language can be verified by direct reference to what can be sensibly observed. If I make a statement about something in this world, it can be validated by the observation of that entity or occurrence. But religious language, because it refers to the transcendent and unobservable, cannot be validated in this way. Hence we face the problem of how we communicate the Christian message to a world which has its sight and language limited to a this-worldly perspective. We have to justify God-talk and also employ it so as to make our message intelligible. In a naturalistic and secular world, we need carefully to examine the issue of communication. This means looking for a new hermeneutic.

God-Talk and the Disclosure of the Christ-Event

We have been through a difficult period so far as religious language is concerned. An intensive examination of the nature and possible validity of language across the past decades has slowly resulted in the emancipation of language from a naturalistic straightjacket. The naturalistic challenge to religious language is another dimension of the belief that scientific method is the only way to certain and reliable knowledge. Language can only be meaningful if it can be verified, as can all scientific statements, at the level of sensible observation. Once language endeavors to describe what cannot be seen, touched and handled, it moves into the realm of nonsensical statements. Language about moral behavior can only be meaningful when we omit references to transcendent claims and abstract ideals and, instead, examine how such behavior has survival value. As for language which refers to God and the supernatural, that can never possess meaning, for it is not subject to empirical verification. God cannot be examined under a microscope or viewed through a telescope. He has no body like finite persons—this by religious definition. When we say that he is love, this cannot be empirically tested, since he has no body and since love is associated with a visibie mode of bodily behavior. The whole thesis of this has been the premise that there is only one legitimate cognitive use of language, and that is when it refers to what can be sensed. Other uses of language convey no knowledge, even though they may express feelings and emotions.

Fortunately we have left this behind, but the process of disentangling ourselves from this attack has left us very aware that we need to define and use religious language more carefully. Religious language contains insights and expresses depths in the divine disclosure which abstract language and prosaic utterance can never express. Deep in religious experience the human imagination is so captured by the Transcendent Presence that it shapes poetic analogies and models to communicate to others the insights which are contained in a particular divine disclosure. Poetry is the natural language of religion, because it is built up of similes and metaphors. It takes images and models from the visible to portray the invisible. It seeks to express ineffable feelings by analogies drawn from more mundane experience. The language of the prophets is full of this. Our Lord himself was a poet. How else can we talk about the Supreme Mystery, the God who surpasses our understanding and who cannot be contained by our earthbound concepts? Great preaching, then, is always allusive. It points. It seeks analogies to make clear some partial unveiling of the final Transcendent Mystery which is God.

This creative imagination, with its poetic dimension, is evident in all forms of the religious consciousness, even the most primitive. Indeed, the most primitive forms of religion disclose how early man told stories about his gods. In these he sought to express his spiritual insights in language which portrayed the deities as personal and their activities in ways akin to very human conduct. Models and dynamic models, analogies and symbols, similes and metaphors are the natural language of religion at all levels. When the supreme revelation of God comes, therefore, as testified to in the biblical records, we must not be surprised if this form of language still persists. Furthermore, we must not try to take the poetry out of it and interpret its models and analogies literally or in more abstract and less allusive language. They are models and analogies because they point beyond their literal referents. What they actually refer to, the Transcendent Presence, is both like and unlike such literal referents, yet there is enough similarity for the model to convey to other persons something of the vision which has been granted to the religious man.

Within the Judeo-Christian disclosure such models of God's nature and activity were shaped in the inspired imagination of prophets and apostles. We may think of the disclosure situation as a kind of Jacob's ladder in which the disclosure of God and the responsive imagination of man met and intermingled like the angels ascending and descending. The result was models grounded in the historical disclosure and embodying insights and truths which our discursive logic is inadequate to express. Those models are given dynamic form in the Christian language which describes God's activity through His Son. We shall call them dynamic models because they tell a story of the divine activity and are not static models which only refer to some aspect of the divine nature. We must note that the models are taken from this-worldly usage and used of the Transcendent. They are thus of the nature of analogies. Jesus is not God's son in the same sense that we have sons, and yet the best qualities of sonship come as near as possible to describe his relationship to the Father. Again, God is not Father in our human finite understanding of fatherhood, yet the best qualities of that human fatherhood point to his innermost nature. We think of the dynamic models or myths associated with Creation, of those associated with the ultimate consummation, including the Son of Man coming on the clouds of heaven, and of the symbolism of the Cross and its sacrifice. There is historical anchorage, and the models have a base in ordinary linguistic usage, but they point beyond this mundane sphere to the transcendent. They describe the nature and activity of the divine Mystery.

This means that our Christian discourse is communicable. At one level it rests on the intramundane level of discourse. Yet such language must not be interpreted literally. It is not univocal. It is analogical. Its words are employed symbolically, and, as such, they point to the Transcendent. I.T. Ramsey suggests that religious language is odd language in the sense that it points beyond any relation it may have to intra-mundane experience. He holds that it is able to point because it adds qualifiers to its models and so prevents them from being taken literally. The description of the divine disclosure in salvation history and the Christ-event also has axiological models or felt analogies. That is to say, it describes the Transcendent Presence in analogies taken from our feelingful responses in intrapersonal and intramundane relationships; but it qualifies them, too, by additions which safeguard against literal interpretation. So we speak not of love but of *almighty* love, not of creation but of creation *out of nothing*, not of cause but of *uncaused* cause or *first* cause. God is personal, but he is *infinite* personal being. God exercises moral claim, but it is *absolute* demand. Any hermeneutic of the Christian disclosure requires communication in such a form.

Now the models, static and dynamic, of the biblical testimonies, reflect the culture of their time, for they were conceived in the imagination of historical persons. Hence there is a primitive *naïveté* in some dynamic models, as for example the creation and fall stories, and certainly an anachronistic garb in all of them. Their insight into divine activity and human response is conveyed in conceptual frameworks which make little contact with modern culture. Yet the insight is what matters, and we cannot dismiss the dynamic models or take away their poetic imagery. We need to remember that the Christian dynamic models serve a symbolic function. They convey insight, and this we dare not destroy. Reinhold Niebuhr has referred to the permanent and transient aspects of such myths. The transient is bound up with an outmoded and often primitive world-structure (*weltbilt*), and such a conceptual framework may well be discarded. The permanent is the continuing revelation of the transcendent, and its symbolism must be retained. What we need, according to Ricoeur, is a mature *naïveté*, a hermeneutic which pays attention to the symbolic role that the dynamic model can still perform. The poetic and analogical form must be retained even though expressed in a more mature garb consistent with modern culture.

This symbolic structure is central in all our theological thinking. As we reflect upon Christian experience and seek to understand the divine disclosure which has been granted to faith, our thinking continually seeks for models which will express the insights contained in the original symbolism associated with the historical disclosure. Thus as we seek to grasp the truth in the original biblical testimony with its symbolism, we have to re-express this truth in secondary models which make the faith more intelligible to our world. Our major problem in preaching is to find such models which still convey the original disclosure. As one Catholic friend said to me, the present theological crisis is, in part, a crisis about theological models.

We preachers must take note of this. Remember how Lewis Carroll expresses our dilemma in *Through the Looking Glass*. The White Queen says to Alice: "I'm just one hundred and one, five months and a day." Alice says: "I can't believe *that*." "Can't you," replies the Queen, "Try again, draw a long breath, and shut your eyes." As secular man listens to some of our preaching, he often reacts in the same way. Our language is so anachronistic, our models are so outmoded, that he dismisses what we say as incredible.

One good illustration of this is at the very center of our preaching to a secular society—the problem of interpreting transcendence to a one-tier culture from which ideas of the supernatural and the thought of a two-tier universe have been banished. The biblical symbolism of height has lost its significance in an infinite universe. There is occasional use of the symbol of depth, and this certainly becomes more appropriate in days when *depth* psychology obviously has symbolic and not a literal significance in the understanding of human behavior. God can be thought of as the deep that couches beneath.

But a much more appropriate model might be found at the level of finite personhood. The disclosure in the Christ-event is of God as a self-giving personal being, and many of the biblical models for God picture him in personal terms—as Father, Creator, King, etc. Now, it is significant of man that he is self-transcendent. He is a free being able to rise above his personal structures and direct them. He is in time, and yet, in his self-awareness, he is able to remember his past and anticipate his future in decisions grounded in his freedom in the present moment. He is able to be self-aware and to transcend his bodily and mental structures. Yet he also pervades the whole. We may take this as a model for the divine transcendence. Let us picture God as the personal depth of this universe, who yet pervades its whole structure as an immanent presence. Because it is an analogy, such a model must not be taken literally, for the world is not God's body; it exists by his sustaining word above an abyss of nothingness. God is the personal self-transcendent depth of the universe. Here is yet one more model by which to communicate the biblical insights .

The preacher will continually strive to create a new hermeneutic by which to communicate the disclosure of the Christ-event to his day. He will present his message coherently, using his models to make the disclosure intelligible to secular man. He will use his understanding of the disclosure to cast light on every human experience. He will endeavor to show that the Christ-event gives wider meaning to history and a deeper understanding to the world-structure which science presents. But always he will be pointing through all this to the transcendent mystery, the hidden God who yet discloses himself through his creatures and supremely in Jesus the Christ.

Such a God is always mystery. A little girl was asked how she drew her pictures. Her reply was: "First I think and then I draw a line around my think." We preachers cannot do that with God. Our models, symbols, and myths cannot contain him. All we can do is point, for he bursts the bounds of all our language. His ways are finally past finding out.

The emphasis on the disclosure in the Christ-event is a reminder that we preachers have an empirical base. It is true that our experience of the Christ is not such that we can share it as something which others may sensibly observe. What we say about Jesus is not open to empirical verification in the narrow sense of empirical. But we do have something concrete to which to point, a historical life, death and resurrection. The disclosure comes through these occurrences and transforms them into revelatory and redemptive events. Now, the disclosure means the discerning of a certain pattern and depth in the occurrences. It comes through the empirically observable insofar as we can speak of the historical past in such terms. It certainly came to the first eyewitnesses in this way. But it transcends the empirically observable and thus is not subject to empirical verification. All that we can do is point to the Christ-event with our symbolic and mythical language. We hope thereby that others will become aware of the transcendent depth and its disclosure. Preaching ultimately points to the Christ and hopes that its words will evoke a disclosure situation for the hearers. As the preacher bears his testimony and points to the Incarnate Presence with models, symbols, and myths that have contact with the experience of secular man, the Christ-event becomes contemporaneous with those who hear, and the Transcendent Presence creates a disclosure situation.

A traveler was lost in the mists of the Welsh mountains. He wandered for hours seeking a way down. At last, weary and on the verge of despair, he heard a voice coming through the mist: "I wonder if by any chance he has gone this way." So to secular man, wandering and lost in the misty confusion of this secular city, looking for meaning and security, there comes a Word from beyond, a disclosure of a redeeming Presence. Of that Word we preachers are the bearers.

The Preacher's Immediate Environment

The Worship of the Believing Community

Evelyn Underhill defined worship as "an acknowledgement of Transcendence; that is to say, of a Reality independent of the worshipper, which is always more or less deeply coloured by mystery, and which is there first" (*Worship* [New York: Harper & Brothers, 1936], p. 3). If, through preaching, the Transcendent communicates itself, it follows that preaching and worship belong together and that preaching requires worship as its setting.

Worship is indeed a divine-human dialogue in which both God and man are involved. The human approach to God, which is one significant dimension of worship, requires as its counterpart that divine approach to man which is brought to a focus in the preaching of the Word and the Sacrament of the Bread and Wine. Of course, even our preaching has both dimensions in it, for it is both an act of God in which the hearers are confronted with the Gospel and also an act of man in which the preacher offers his confession of faith to God. As P. T. Forsyth so wisely put it: "The sermon is the Word of the gospel returning in confession to the God who gave it. It is addressed to men indeed, but in truth it is offered to

God. Addressed to men but offered to God—that is the true genius of preaching" (*Positive Preaching and the Modern Mind* [London: Independent Press, 1957], p. 66). We shall need to elaborate this further, for preaching is also an act of the whole believing community, a confession of its faith. As such, preaching becomes an act of communion in which God and worshippers commune through the Word of the gospel audibly confessed by the preacher.

Man's chief end is "glorify God and enjoy Him for ever." In other words, man's final destiny is the worship of God, for he was created to commune with God and reflect back to God something of God's glory. He was made to walk with Yahweh in the garden and to bear the divine image. This is the picture of the Genesis stories of creation. Now, if the Church is the community of the redeemed, of those who have been set free in Christ to realize their true destiny, the central function of the church is to worship God, to glorify Him and enjoy Him forever. Indeed, if we think of the Church as a witnessing and evangelizing community, its true task is to extend the worship of God to all men and all creatures. The eschatological vision sees the Christ as summing up all things in Himself. As we have suggested, this implies that the incarnation of the Christ is extended through the Church to the whole universe so that "God becomes all in all". Such an eschatological vision implies that the Church's task is to witness to God in such a way that all men and, indeed, all the creation shall be led to glorify God and enjoy Him forever. Worship becomes the center of the Church's life and the objective of its mission.

It seems hardly necessary to point out that so much turns upon the attitude of the worshipper. Because he is often not called upon to participate actively in the liturgical setting, except in hymn singing and occasionally in responses, it is easy for him to develop an attitude of detachedness. He may look upon the liturgical practices as an observer rather than participate in them as a worshipper. A prevalent disease in our generation is "spectatoritis," the habit of looking on at things. It has spread from the realm of sports and the movies to many other realms as well. It has swollen to gigantic proportions, thanks to television. Indeed, one wonders how long it will take us to develop a new biological mutation with telescopic eyes and flapping ears. It has certainly got inside our church doors. In church, men and women watch the minister and listen to the choir with little active participation in prayer or praise. In the thirties there appeared on a church bulletin board a very unfortunate juxtaposition:

> Preacher next Sunday: Rev. Ebenezer Tomkinson
> Subject: What Are We To Do About the World Depression?
> Anthem: Search me, O God.

We may laugh, but unintentionally that notice touches the spot. Our worship can be a dead thing, leaving us floundering and bewildered in a changing world. Equally it can be a living power in our lives, providing us with a sense of direction and a freshness of vision. Everything turns upon two things. One is the quality of the preaching. but even the best of sermons may fail without a responsive attitude in the worshippers. This is the other issue—the state of our own spirits, whether we suffer from "spectatoritis" or whether we are worshipping in sincerity and in truth.

The Nature and Aim of Worship

The primary aim of worship must always be communion with God. In the words of the catechism, already cited, "Man's chief end is to know God and to enjoy Him forever."

Worship, in its basic meaning, is concerned with the acknowledging of "worth-ship." It is ascribing supreme worth to God. Thus it is fundamentally bound up with our priorities. When Paul Tillich defines religious faith as a state of being ultimately concerned, he is emphasizing this basic aspect of worship. By ultimate concern he means that which involves the totality of a person's being, "the structure, the meaning, and the aim of existence" (*Systematic Theology*, vol. I, [Chicago: University of Chicago Press,, 1951], p. 14). What has ultimate and final priority for us is that which has power both to threaten and to save our total being. This is the ultimate ground of all being and meaning. At the end of man's quest for existence, for meaning, for true selfhood, for being, stands God.

The urge to worship is an integral part of man's nature. He was made to worship, as the sparks are prone to fly upwards. He cannot escape God, for if he does not worship the living God, he will find a surrogate, a false ultimate concern around which he can build his existence and give it meaning. We have already noted this in the propensity of Americans to develop civil religion in which God is dressed in American garb, becomes identified with our cultural values, and is regarded as the guardian of our lifestyle with its prejudices and distorted relationships. But then we can erect a race into the place of God, as did Hitler with his creed of the blood, the race and the soil. We can worship the "proletariat," for Marxism is a perverted form of religion. Such false religions have their cult symbols and liturgical practices—the Nazi Swastika, the tomb of Lenin, the American flag. Of course, we can even worship our possessions or our family. You may remember the prayer: "Bless me, my wife, my son John and his wife, us four, and no more. Amen." This touches us all, for we who worship the living God can so limit and restrict him in our own thoughts and attitudes that we inhibit the working of his grace in our lives. Our worship can be almost a mockery.

Worship is thus not a human discovery, but an inborn urge, a divine creation in the human soul. God has made us so that we need to live in relation to him if we are to be real persons. Without him we lose our final security and basic meaning. Thus the urge to worship is bound up with the primary need for security and meaning. Because of that, if we do not worship the living God, then we shall worship race, state, nature, humanity, or material possessions. The impulse to worship which God has implanted drives us to find surrogates for him. Such an impulse only finds its fulfillment and satisfaction in the conscious apprehension of a supremely adorable being with whom we have a deep affinity.

This means that God is ever there drawing us back to himself, for he has put eternity in our hearts. Even when we build our lives around false gods, choose wrong priorities and direct our existence by pseudoultimate concerns, God is still operating in judgment and in mercy. The objective reality of the God of worship has been denied by many thinkers who find the root of religion and worship in human need and insecurity. Ever since Feuerbach, there have been those who base worship, not on a God-implanted urge with its concomitant need, but solely on a basic human insecurity. They have argued that it is not God who creates man but man who creates God. Beset by a hostile environment and feeling his own insecurity, man projects his need for security upon the backdrop of the universe. He creates a God who will image his ideal self, a human nature freed from the limitations and purified from the distortions which beset individual persons. Thus religion is man relating himself to himself, and worship is man trying to satisfy his needs by bowing down before his own ideal image. It is a purely subjective experience. To quote Feuerbach: "God is my hidden, my assured existence; he is the subjectivity of subjects, the personality of persons" (trans. George Eliot, *The Essence of Christianity* [New York: Harper Torchbooks, 1957], p. 174).

In more recent days, we find Freud teaching a similar viewpoint in his psychological analysis. For him, "man, disappointed in and frustrated by the failure of his earthly father, projects the father image upon the backdrop of the universe and finds consolation in the worship and contemplations of this ideal figure" (E. C. Rust, *Positive Religion in a Revolutionary Time* [Philadelphia: Westminster Press, 1970], p. 128). Religion and worship become matters of wish fulfillment. In a parallel way, Marx reduces worship to an economic base. Religion is "dope for the people," a soporific by which the economically deprived, the have-nots, are persuaded that their needs will be met and their lot righted in the "sweet by and by." Worship is concerned with a fictitious "pie in the sky." Thereby, their attention is directed away from the absence of pies in the here and now. We preachers in the pulpit, need to remember that such ideas may find a lodging place in the minds of some of our hearers.

Such needs as these thinkers enumerate are often secondary, and yet they are expressions of that basic insecurity which is bound up with the urge to worship. They do not create religious faith, but they do condition it. Our worship is always conditioned by the life situation in which we express our desire for the living God. Our needs provide the conditions under which our inborn urge to worship is awakened. As we become aware of ourselves, our limitations and frailty, our finitude and insufficiency, we also become aware of the infinite presence. As Schleiermacher saw, self-awareness is also awareness of the Other. Such self-awareness brings with it a sense of need, of insecurity, and it is within such a conditioning experience that the desire to worship finds expression. You may remember the story of the old lady on a transatlantic liner in the midst of a heavy storm. Alarmed and fearful, she approached the captain. "Captain," she asked, "will the ship be wrecked? Are we in danger of sinking?" "Lady," he replied, "You see those sailors over there. So long as they are cursing and swearing, you are safe. But when they begin to pray, put on your life belt." But such is only the vestibule to true worship. Men worship God finally because they have been encountered by an infinite supremely adorable Presence who demands their total allegiance.

We preachers need to remember this, however, for so often we present religion at this lower level and confine a service of worship to a picture of God who is a kind of universal provider. As Pepys once expressed it—the Bible becomes a handy book for a successful merchant. The accusation of many thinking people that religion is an escape mechanism and that worship is a refuge from facing life's brute realities is sometimes well-founded. Finally, the word of God which we proclaim is concerned to disclose an infinitely gracious God whose love meets us at our deepest need, our insecurity and alienation, but who does not thereby satisfy many of our lesser needs or remove the problems that perturb our spirits. Rather he gives us the grace to have the right attitude toward them, the courage to wrest a finer victory out of seeming defeat, the sense of his accompanying and reinforcing Presence. We do not create that Word of God out of our needs by some supreme act of imagination. It meets us where we are, and it is that encounter with God which answers our urge to worship and brings it to full flower.

The history of Christian worship shows how God, not man's need, comes to occupy the center of the stage. Every liturgy shows both the hills and the valleys, with alternating emphasis on God's love and glory and on man's need, yet the final emphasis falls on the divine. Finally it is he who draws us to his presence; it is his glory before which we bow; it is the majesty of his love which makes us forget all other things beside, including our needs. The divine wonder, beauty and majesty should be central, and our needs are but the vestibule to his Presence. This should be the shape of the worship in which our preaching is set.

So our worship is our response to the divine Presence. It is our human attempt to offer to God something that shall be worthy of his majesty and grace. It expresses the deep truth that we can never enjoy fellowship unless we offer to him a perfect and acceptable sacrifice of our lives in obedience, in penitence, and in devotion. Before the Creator we cannot draw near and commune unless we offer ourselves, and worship expresses that offering. This need to commune through self-offering is basic to our being, a mark of our creaturehood, a root of that fundamental *angst* of which our contemporary existentialists make so much. William Temple has stated this meaning of worship in well-chosen words:

> Worship is the submission of all our nature
> to God. It is the quickening of the conscience
> by His holiness; the nourishment of the mind with
> His truth; the purifying of imagination by His
> beauty; the opening of the heart to His love; the
> surrender of the will to His purpose—and all this
> gathered up in adoration, the most selfless
> emotion of which our nature is capable and therefore
> the chief remedy for that self-centeredness which is

our original sin and the source of all actual sin.
(*Readings in St. John's Gospel*
[London: Macmillan; 1945], p. 68).

It makes all the difference for us as ministers whether we think of the Church service as something we prepare for man or as something which, in the name and spirit of Jesus Christ, we lay upon the altar of God. Worship is our imperfect oblation in the presence of God, and above all else we need a God-consciousness in the conduct of worship, in the preaching of the Word and in the administration of the Sacraments. It is only as we focus all our thoughts and feelings upon the divine that we shall be able to lead our people into the eternal Presence. We must remember that preaching is only to be understood within the totality of worship. It functions truly only as that totality is both permeated with a consciousness of God's presence and characterized as a communal offering in the eternal sacrifice of Jesus Christ our Lord.

The Theological Base of Christian Worship
Central in Christian worship, as in Christian preaching, is the Christ, his life, death and resurrection, Jesus as the historicity of God.

First of all, Christian worship means the worship of the God and Father of our Lord Jesus Christ. Our knowledge of God centers in the historical disclosure of the glory of God in the face of Jesus Christ. For us, God is no impersonal absolute transcending history. He has drawn near to men in the person of his Son and revealed himself in a sequence of historical events. This is not just what we proclaim in our preaching; it colors every aspect of our worship. The totality of our liturgy should be permeated by the reality of the divine disclosure and act in Jesus. In prayers and praises it should point to him.

For, in the second place, our approach to God is conditioned, not only by what the Christ reveals, but also by what he has done. Indeed, the activity of the Christ is integral to and a central part of his revelation. If there is any truth that is evident in our Christian tradition it is the fallen and sinful nature of humanity. Of himself man is not worthy to approach God. The urge to worship is turned upon himself, upon the idols he creates, upon nature, upon humanity. As William Temple reminded us, in the passage just quoted, his original sin and the source of all his actual sin is his self-centeredness. He has an urge for communion with God, but that basic need has become so distorted and perverted by his self-centeredness that he is not worthy to approach God. There is a radical twist in his personality, so that he is never capable of offering that totality of surrender, that perfect sacrifice, which is the precondition of communion. His worship is always imperfect, for the offering of his own life is never clear of his self-seeking. Selfishness and greed are present even in the innermost sanctuary. For even in worship our pride may lead us to build our own way to heaven like the builders of the Tower of Babel. "I am just and live peaceably with my neighbour. What more can God require?" Though not so blantantly as this, such an attitude of complacency can be with us and with out congregation.

Sin is the innermost problem of humanity. God has made us for himself, but we have misused our freedom and are not worthy of his fellowship. From this we cannot escape except God Himself deliver us. And he has created the conditions whereby we may draw near. In the self-giving of Jesus, culminating in his Cross, our sin and pride are met in one supreme act of divine grace. God accepts the perfect sacrifice of our humanity in the person of his Son, and through that sacrifice of perfect penitence and obedience we ourselves may draw near. Here is the mystery which transcends every mystery. God is at once High Priest and Victim. He accepts the sacrifice, and he *is* the sacrifice. God was in Christ reconciling us to himself, doing what we in our sin and pride could never do, making it possible for us to enter into fellowship with himself. As we have noted in an earlier chapter, this is the supreme paradox of our faith.

This means that the sole basis of our worship is not our merit but our faith. We draw near because of God's amazing love disclosed in Jesus, and our sacrifice of worship becomes effective, not by its own perfection, but because it is offered through Jesus Christ our Lord. Without our union with Him in faith, our worship is of no avail. It is by grace that we are saved, and that not of ourselves, it is the free gift of God. Man is not worthy to know God. It is God's redemptive act that alone makes man fit to stand in the divine presence and to offer his gift.

In the presence of Christ, then, we know that we cannot make a reasonable offering of ourselves in worship unless He enables us to do so. "We cannot offer our best gift or the right gift unless we first receive the divine gift." It is only when, by faith, we make ourselves one with the Crucified that we may draw near and drink of the water of eternal life. Then our offering becomes a part of His perfect oblation, and our imperfections are covered by his sinless splendor. In the Genevan Service

Order this truth is expressed: "Wherefore, O Lord, renouncing ourselves and abandoning all other hope, we flee to this precious covenant by which our Lord Jesus Christ, offering His own Body to thee in sacrifice, has reconciled us to thee. Look, therefore, O Lord, not on us but on the face of Christ, that by His intercession thy anger may be appeased, and thy face may shine forth upon us for our joy and our salvation. . . ."

In the words of Bright's hymn:

> Look, Father, look on his anointed face,
> And only look on us as found in Him.
> Look not on our misusings of thy grace,
> Our prayer so languid, and our faith so dim.
> For, lo, between our sins and their reward
> We set the passion of Thy Son, Our Lord.

In Christian worship the primitive motive of fear in the presence of the numinous has developed into humility, adoration and awe before God's supreme act of grace. God's love sweeps down into our hearts in Christ, and in Him we draw near. "We love Him because He first loved us." Or, in the words of Augustine, "Thou wast at the helm though very secretly." In worship, our theology is translated into action. Indeed, worship expresses that experience of God's grace which theology endeavors to interpret. The Church lives not by its ideas and its creeds alone, but by the grace of God mediated through His Spirit in its act of worship. You may remember the picture drawn by Gregory of Nyssa: "Constantinople is full of mechanics and slaves who are all of them profound theologians. If you desire a man to change a piece of silver he informs you wherein the Son differs from the Father; if you ask the price of a loaf you are told by way of reply that the Son is inferior to the Father; and if you inquire whether the bath is ready, the answer is that the Son was made out of nothing. . . ." Finally the dogma only lives when it is expressed in the cultus.

A theology finds its significance when it finds practical enactment in the worship of a Christian community. The dry bones of doctrine are translated into life by worship. That is why there is value in the keeping of the Christian Year. It helps us to bring our Christian worship into line with the full sweep of Christian revelation and Christian truth, and to incorporate every aspect of Christian experience and dogma within our worshipful approach to God. A service of worship will, indeed, use every device available to present the Gospel to men and evoke a worshipful response to God. The symbols of cup and bread employed in the Lord's supper, the cross upon the communion table, the burial in the baptismal waters, the Christian symbols sometimes portrayed on banners—all serve to dramatize the Christian revelation and to make the historic event of redemption a contemporaneous experience.

It has been said that our worship is impoverished if it is limited to one aspect of the Godhead only. This is true especially of the Holy Spirit. Without His mediating presence, the Church and the Worship alike would lose their vital meaning, and yet, only too often, He remains obscured both in thought and in worship. Whitsuntide needs to be resuscitated in our Church life, and its full and rich significance made plain. That significance can only become real if, in our worship, we plead for a fresh outpouring of God's Spirit on all flesh. We need, even in the Sacrament of the Lord's Supper, to make the ministry of the Spirit central. The Epiclesis, or invocation of the Spirit on the elements, is one part of the primitive communion rites which we have too sadly forgotten.

The Dialogic Pattern of Communion with God

True worship involves a two-fold aspect. As was suggested earlier, it is like Jacob's ladder, with the angels ascending and descending upon it. There is a two-way traffic between the human soul and God. Man acts, but so also does God; and, without the outgoing of divine grace, the human oblation would be of little avail. We enter into communion with God because God, of His mercy, comes out to us, and such communion is possible only because God has Himself created the redeeming conditions in Jesus Christ our Lord. We come believing that God's presence is offered us in Christ, and, by faith in Christ, we enter into fellowship with Him. All worship is essentially Christocentric. In Christ we may draw near to God, and through Christ God draws near to us. He is the mediator of divine fellowship.

This two-fold aspect may be expressed in the words of P. T. Forsyth when he states that "prayer is a gift and a sacrifice that we make: sacrament is a gift and a sacrifice that God makes. In prayer we go to God: in sacrament God comes to us." Thus our service of worship necessarily falls into two parts. The first consists of our own prayer and praise. The second consists of the two means of grace—the Preaching of the Word and the Sacrament of the Lord's Table. Let us consider these in turn.

In the first we symbolize and express the offering of our whole lives to God. In the reading of the Word, God's divine act in Christ is brought before us, and out of the realization of that redeeming grace spring our adoration, our thanksgiving, our petition, our intercession, our praise, and our confession. The essence of worship is the complete offering of self before the love and splendor of God in Christ. Because of this, in all our prayer and praise, the emphasis is not on ourselves, our own comfort and security, but on God's glory and purpose. Worship expresses our total dependence on the free action of the living God. In this we focus our attention on God's love and on God's purpose for our lives.

Yet worship also mediates the self-giving of God. It brings to men that divine gift by which they are empowered to make the offering of their own lives to God. Something happens in worship. God acts as well as man. In the preached Word, God's Spirit confronts men with the Living Truth, and, by their response to that truth, they are judged and saved. Preaching is the medium by which God's Saving Word goes out to men, and those who worship can never be the same after they have heard that Word. Do we preachers verily believe that? Do we believe that even though there be little outward response, yet preaching in the Spirit never returns unto God void? The preached word may be filled and charged with divine authority. This act of human speech becomes an event pregnant with God's grace and power. In it we are brought face to face with God Himself. It is the earthly vessel in which God wills to come to men. So he who hears God's Word without "hearing" it stands under judgment. Its utterance brings salvation and disaster. It may not be heard with impunity. To him who lets it speak to him the Word becomes a light upon the way and nourishing food.

This divine gift finds its other medium in the Lord's Supper. Here God's Word is not spoken but acted, and through the symbolism of the feast his grace is offered to men. The Eucharist is no mere sign, no bare remembrance of the past, no mere symbolism in which the death of the Lord is brought back to men's minds. It conveys that of which it speaks. In and through it there is offered to men that grace which was released by the historical work of Christ. The Sacrament does not add anything to the victory of Calvary, but it does make it effective in the life of the worshipper. It is a means of grace, so that, as Calvary is portrayed in word and symbol, the free gift of eternal life descends upon men. Just as the score of Beethoven's Fifth Symphony is the means whereby the music is made effective to successive generations of hearers, so the symbolic acts of breaking the bread and blessing the cup are the essential factors whereby, down through the years, God's grace may be conveyed to those who partake. At the same time, the Eucharist is only a means of grace on the grounds of faith. It is not *ex opere operato*. Grace is not a shot of spiritual blood-plasm which is injected into men by their partaking of the elements. It is a gift of divine fellowship, love, and power mediated to men through the symbolic elements, but dependent always upon their receptive faith. As Augustine wrote: *"Believe* and thou hast eaten the sacraments.

The Corporate Concern of Christian Worship

The corporate aim of Christian worship is the creation and sustaining of a divine community. The Christian cannot fulfil his spiritual obligations in solitude. He is a part of a social complex, and none of his devotions can be performed without relation to that complex. What is more, he is a member of a Christian community, and to that community his private worship must bear some relationship. In this discussion we are considering, not his private, but his public worship, and this is immediately a corporate business. Here we do something in common with others. We act, not as individuals, but as a community, and the total act of worship is not just the sum of the mere individual acts. Here we are members of the mystical Body of Christ. We act as an organic unity, and we may firmly believe that the individual receives something spiritual by his relation to the fellowship, something which he does not and cannot attain in private devotion. Something new is added to the consciousness of each individual by the consciousness of the group, rich in traditions, memories and association, whilst God's grace working through the fellowship enriches the individual life in a way impossible to the solitary worshipper. For one thing, by sharing in the life and action of the Church, the believer places his emphasis not on himself but on the fellowship, so that his own selfish needs are lost in the remembrance of the Body of Christ. Indeed, a true measure of our worship would be how far we have become immersed in the fellowship.

This means that true Christian worship can never be the act of the individual alone, but of the whole organism. In it the whole group lifts its sacrifice to God, each individual contributing his or her share. Psychologically this helps the worshipper, but spiritually it is of still more fundamental importance. For a corporate act of worship is an expression of that life of love to which God has called us in Christ and which is the immediate result of our having communion with Him. To commune with God, to experience the divine forgiveness and grace, is to die to the self and to rise again into the life of the Christian fellowship. Someone has said: "Corporate worship is an education in love and a purgation of egoism." Our corporate response to God's redeeming grace in Christ embraces a fully balanced richness which the individual alone could not attain. Frere, in *The Principles of Religious Ceremonial*, writes: "The ideal was that each person should contribute something to the whole . . . and it is not too much to say that without any doubt this is the only true ideal of Christian worship."

The truth is that we are saved by Christ into a fellowship, and that communion with God means the love of the brethren. Hence, no worship can be full and rich which is not also a corporate act. Nor can our sacrifice be wholly acceptable in Christ unless it be the sacrifice of individual lives lived in a community of love, and therefore of the community as a whole. Christian worship should be the living utterance of the life of the Church. The downsweep of eternal life at Pentecost carried the individual disciples into a worshipping community, and full communion with God is impossible unless it be in an act of worship in which I commune with my brother also. Whatever our conception of the Church, it remains true that *extra ecclesiam nulla salus*.

The Church is not just a gathering. It is the Body of Christ. We have seen already that our approach to God is only through Christ, and one aspect of this truth is that we can approach God only as members of the mystical Body of Christ. Did not our Lord imply this when he said that we could not love God and hate our brother? We can approach God only in the fellowship, and our individual and personal worship gains significance only as we relate to it to the Christian community.

It is here that we gain a real understanding of the High Priesthood of Christ. It is not we who pray in the vision of Heaven, but Christ who kneels before the Father making our approach real and authentic. We are but the knees with which His Body touches this gross earth. To approach in Christ means to approach as His Body, through Christ as our Head, and all corporate worship is such an act of the Church.

This common act is seen especially in the Communion Service. There is little doubt that, in the early days of the Church and in the more primitive liturgies, the Eucharist was regarded as a corporate act of the Church. Thus the offertory act became a concerted act in which the whole Body of Christ offered itself afresh to God through its Head. When Calvary was symbolically reenacted in the breaking of the bread and the blessing of the cup, the whole Church, by faith, incorporated itself in this mystery and drew near in the crucified Lord. When, in the Epiclesis, the presence of the Holy Spirit was invoked, this was a prayer not only for the sanctification of the elements but also for the sanctification of the communicants. If the bread was symbolical of the broken body of the Lord, were not they the Body of the Lord? So, in the breaking of the Bread, the Church offered itself in the sacrifice of Christ, and, in the pouring out of the cup, the Church poured out its own life as an imperfect oblation which Christ's sacrifice had made perfect. The Eucharist involved the sacrifice of the Church as the whole Body of Christ incorporate. In it, Paul's two senses of the Body of Christ were allowed to run together—so that when the elements were broken, poured out and blessed, and the offering of Calvary preached afresh, there was linked with this the actual offering up of His Body which is the Church. It was this that led Augustine to declare in one of his sermons: "Since you are the Body of Christ and His Members, it is the mystery of yourselves which lies upon the Lord's Table: it is the mystery of yourselves which you receive."

With the passage of time this corporate emphasis was lost, and the individual went to the sacrament to appropriate grace for himself. Thus, for Thomas à Kempis, communion meant the meeting of the individual Christian with the heavenly Lord and Friend. As the Roman Catholic doctrine of the mass took the place of the symbolic rite, and it was crudely believed that Calvary was actually celebrated afresh, the priest alone made the sacrifice, the congregation became spectators, and extraliturgical devotions were encouraged during the mass, since the worshippers could not themselves actively participate. Unfortunately, this emphasis has remained in the modern Evangelical view of the Sacrament.

In reality, the element of fellowship is indispensable for a true approach to the communion service. The service is an act of the fellowship, in which we offer ourselves afresh as Christ's Body as, through the symbols, the Cross is preached to us, and in which we together are nourished by the same food. God's grace is mediated through the elements on the grounds of faith, but its outgoing is to the building up of the Body. The sacrament exists to integrate us into the fellowship and to strengthen the bonds of love between the members. In it God's life is given to us in terms of sharing. The seed has died to give the bread. The grape has bled to yield the wine. So, too, God's love is given through the death of Christ, and as it is given in Christ, it must be shared in His Body which is the Church. We who together eat the Bread of Life are built up into one community by so doing. "As this broken bread was scattered upon the mountains and being gathered together became one, so may Thy Church be gathered together from the ends of the earth into Thy Kingdom; and, as this wine was gathered from the fruit of the vine, so may all thy people abide as branches of the True Vine, Jesus Christ our Lord, Amen."

"In eating and drinking we join ourselves to Christ's sacrificial act in the most intimate way possible. To each other as one body, feeding by faith in our hearts upon His body and blood." (W. Robinson: *A Companion to the Communion Service* [London: Oxford University Press, 1942], p. 42).

As we have already suggested, preaching too is an act of the whole fellowship. We have noted the words of P. T. Forsyth that the preaching of the Gospel is an offering to God. The preacher is presenting the Word to the hearers, and yet, at the same time, he and they are offering their words back to God as a confession of their own faith in and commitment to the saving grace which is being proclaimed. Every preacher knows those moments when his preached Word "takes wing." He knows that the congregation is with him, that their hearts and consciences have been stirred and moved by the Word. He should prepare his sermon as a worthy offering to God. He should pray that as he speaks, the fire of the Word will set the congregation aflame, so that he and they can lift the message of the Gospel back to the God who gave it. In Forsyth's words: "Addressed to men but offered to God—that is the true genius of preaching."

This creation and sustaining of a fellowship is thus an aim of worship involved in its primary aim of communion with God. The two are indeed one. In common worship, that fellowship finds its richest expression since it is a fellowship in and through Christ. Through corporate worship the unity of the fellowship is attained, since prayer draws us together in common adoration of the universal Saviour. The members of the Church are bound together in a unity of prayer, and that unity cannot be broken even by the fierce exigencies of life. All Christians are one as they kneel before the altar of God and plead, in their sin, the amazing sacrifice of Christ. There the sinful barriers that divide are broken down, and the pride of man that separates him from his fellows is humbled in the dust.

Consider these words from a significant section in A. G. Hébert's *Liturgy and Society*, entitled "What I learnt in the House of God."

The Church meets on the Lord's Day to offer the Holy
Sacrifice,
using universal symbols, bread and wine,
proclaiming therewith God's redeeming love in Christ:
    'This is My Body which is given for you; take, eat.'
    'This is My Blood of the Covenant; drink ye all of
    this.'
In eating and drinking at the Table of the Lord
    the brethren of the family, my neighbour and I,
    are shown as reconciled with Him
        and in Him with one another:
God has a meaning for our lives, singly and all together:
'What I do thou knowest not now, but thou shalt know
hereafter.'
Here we see that the root of all evil is Godlessness,
    practical Godlessness,
    the exaltation of the self,
    the claim of the self to live as it pleases without God.
Here we see the root of all evil in ourselves
    and confess and are absolved:
    'Thou hast broken my bonds in sunder.'
Thanks be to Him who hath redeemed us and continues
    to save us
    out of this Godlessness,
    into the common life which is in Him,
    into the universal spiritual family and Kingdom,
And has promised the perfecting of this salvation and
    fellowship in the life everlasting.
Glory be to God for all things. Amen.
        (A. G. Hébert, *Liturgy and Society*
        [London: Faber & Faber, 1935], pp. 235-36.

This means that our worship should express and interpret the corporate life of the Christian community. The pattern of Christian worship should proclaim what the Church really is, and in it the members should learn together the common meaning of their life in Christ.

Finally, in and through its worship, the Christian community not only renews the sacrifice of its corporate life and of the lives of its members, but also draws afresh upon resources of divine grace and the springs of eternal life. Only by so doing does it remain the Body of the Lord, and not sink to the level of any earthly society. It is by its worship, by the preaching of the Word and by the celebration of the Sacrament that the Church lives and remains a supernatural and redeemed community in the world of men.

The Individual and Social Aspects of Such Corporate Worship

For the individual, corporate worship means the gathering up of his whole life into the stream of God's kingdom. In corporate worship we present our own lives to God, and this means the dedication of all that we do in this world of space and time. As somebody has said, "Worship should be a 'health service' for soul and for body, giving the fresh air of heaven to intensify the joys and pleasures of life." So, in our Church services, we make use of the common things of daily life, and paradoxically unite them with the transcendent and the eternal. We use bread and wine; we eat and drink before God; thereby family dinner becomes a holy meal. We read aloud and sing in chorus, so that literature and music alike may become sacraments of His presence. We worship before a Cross of wood or iron to remind ourselves that the things upon which we spend our labor may yet be mediums of the fellowship of the Crucified. Dr. John Brown tells how Thackeray and two friends were walking out one night near Edinburgh, while the red sun was setting over the hills. They came to a quarry from which a builder's crane stood up, with its crossbeams in relief against the evening sky, lit by the dying splendor of the sun. They stood for a moment gazing at it, while the same thought struck them all, finding expression in one whispered word: "Calvary." Our worship should be doing that—gathering up our daily task so that we see it in the light of the Cross!

Our worship, then, should make the everyday service of God possible, both by bringing the daily things of life into the light of eternity, and by opening up for us the resources of eternal grace. It should express the application of the Kingdom to every aspect of human life, so that in our prayers the whole of life is brought near to God, always with reference to the corporate relationships of Christ's Church. Our Christian worship should thus weave every detail of our daily routine into our relationship with God; it should include and harmonize all phases of our human experience.

Yet such a dedication of life is only possible if, through his worship, a man appropriates the divine gift of love and power. The act of worship, whilst it is an offering, is also the opening up of heart and mind to the divine goodness and love so that they may enter into us and possess us. To worship is to enter into the Pauline experience that we live, yet not we, but Christ lives in us. As by faith we identify ourselves with Him in our approach to God, so also by faith we open our lives to eternal life through Him. He mediates to us the life of God, or, more truly, He lifts us up into Himself so that, at the highest level, we live in and by Him. Such intimate union with God in Christ is the finest outcome of our worship. It is the individual aspect of that truth we have already considered, viz., that the Church is no earthly community but the mystical Body of the Lord, a supernatural society sustained by the grace of God in Christ, feeding on His broken body and drinking of His outpoured life. The means of grace, by which the life of the Church is maintained, bring to the individual Christian the power and love that he needs. We would not, of course, limit his communion with Christ to such occasions, nor rob his private devotions of their enriching and empowering significance. We are merely pointing out how corporate worship may affect his living.

But, just because we are social, such a lifting up of the individual life implies the lifting up of the structure of society, and this is reinforced by the fact that our corporate worship is the expression of the life of the redeemed community. Our worship cannot be separated from our social life, not can our life within the Body of Christ be separated from the wider obligations to society.

The practical concern of worship as communion with God is the total transfiguration of the created order in which we live. The whole social structure needs to be transformed, and the Church's most effective contribution is through its worship and through the outgoing of that worship in the lives of its members. During the past one hundred years, we have lived in an atomistic order of society, the result of the Industrial Revolution . Laissez-faire individualism held sway until the totalitarian state and the capitalistic combine brought in schemes of social reorganization which dealt with men in the mass. Today, the individual has lost his value and been transformed into cannon fodder, or a cog in the economic machine, or the benevolent object of impersonal social planning. We have swung over from individualism to totalitarianism, and the latter may assume good as well as evil forms. The Church is ultimately concerned with persons, but with persons as they are integrated into a common life. Christ saves the individual, but He saves him into a fellowship. The divine new order has been manifested in Christ's Church as a corporate life in which the individual retains his personal value because he is related to his fellow in a fellowship of love. Community is there without the loss of personal value.

Hence, the Church's task is to recreate social life for redeemed men and women. To save the individual and to save society. No adequate and full social life is possible without personal redemption. No social or political programme is of itself sufficient, nor can the Church identify it with the Kingdom of God. The task of the Church is to create those personal relationships of mutual love and service in Christ without which every scheme of social, national, and international reform will fail. It should have a social gospel in the sense that it condemns the evils of society and declares what God's will must be for the communal life of men. But its primary task is the redemption of the individual and his incorporation into the redeemed community.

The deepest contribution that the Church can make to the life of our time is through its own corporate life as the Body of Christ. (In so doing it proclaims individual salvation and social redemption alike.) There is a story of how Francis opened the eyes of one of his friars who had inquired of his master how he was to preach. The saint led him from the monastery gate all through the streets and lanes of the city, and when finally they had arrived back at the gate from which they had set out, the friar exclaimed: "But, Father, when do we begin to preach?" To which Francis replied: "We have been preaching all the time, for except we preach as we walk, the words which we speak will be of no avail." This story may well have its corporate application. It is as true of the Church as of its individual members that its life must express its preached Word. If that be so, this life will find its expression in the worship of the Christian community and, through thatl in a truer and deeper fellowship than the world can supply of itself.

Dean Sperry writes: "The offices of public worship, which so often seem to have nothing to say to the ordering of the brotherhood of man, say everything to it. They say the one thing that redeems all utopian thinking from the charge of idle fancy, that God is the real bond between man and man" (W. L. Sperry, *Reality in Worship* [New York, 1928] p. 166). In that worship the Church can and must lift the world nearer to

God. In the preaching of the Word the mind of Christ is disclosed, and the minds of men are kept alive to the spiritual aspect of the evils of their day. They are seen, not as social evils, but as the results of the corporate sin of humanity. In the General Confession and its equivalent extempore forms, the Christian community shares the common burden of such corporate sin, remembering that it is itself a part of the sinful race. In its intercession, the Church lifts the world nearer to God, and only as we do learn to exercise this priestly office of intercession shall we learn also how to bring our practical contribution for the healing of the world's wounds. As Dr. Milligan has written of the Church: "No act more closely unites her with her Lord than when, vitalised by His life, instructed by His mind, and guided by His Spirit, she pours forth her soul in entreating God's blessing for mankind. She is there indeed the representative of the seeking Saviour. She is there with all the company of Saints before the Altar of God, offering her own life for the life of the world, that the world may be reconciled to God." (O. B. Milligan, *The Ministry of Worship* [London: Oxford University Press, 1941], p. 39). By so doing we unite ourselves with Christ as the agents through whom God can answer our own prayers. The practical outcome of such intercession must ever be the spirit of the Cross. "For their sakes I sanctify myself," said our Lord and walked the way of Calvary. If we pray for a new order, are we prepared to pay the price of that new order among men? If we pray for better housing, are we beginning with our own Church and private property? If we pray for peace, are our individual members withdrawing investments from the armament rings? To intercede means to offer our lives and our corporate life in the service of humankind. To quote Dean Sperry again: "The cup of cold water is the seal of actuality upon the act of worship, giving it the confirmation it otherwise lacks" (*Reality in Worship*, p. 168).

The Church can best help society as it more truly expresses the Spirit of Christ within its own communal life, and that is only possible when its members sacrifice themselves in Him through its corporate worship. Such worship, if it be true to the life of Christ Himself, moves out from the adoration of God to cover the whole of life. It gathers up all our human powers and capacities so that God's spirit may enter into the whole texture of our individual lives and fill up the pattern of the common life in which we share. The true test of worship is whether it does produce such a high tide in the hearts of the Christian community as overflows with cleansing and fruitfulness into homes and fields and schools and business houses and into the many channels of national and international life.

In Laachen there is the burial place of many kings. The reading desk in the pulpit of the royal chapel has a strange fitting. A crucifix conceals a microphone. That is a parable. The Gospel of the grace of God is broadcast through the crucified Son of God. It is what we find in Him that draws us in worship to God's throne, and it is the grace He imparts that strengthens our lives, builds up the fellowship, and transfigures the social order. Through the Cross, His love and grace are still broadcast to the city of man, and in our worship that love and grace are appropriated by our lives. In this, preaching is central, for God is still pleased through such a foolish medium to save those who believe.

Index of Names

Composition was by Mercer Press Services
    interior design by Jane Denslow
    typesetting by Janet Middlebrooks
        typeset on an Addressograph Multigraph Comp/Set Phototypesetter 5404,
        and paginated on an A/M Comp/Set 4510.

Design and production specifications:
    text typeface—Garamond (11 on 13); display type—Gothic Outline
    text paper 60 pound Glatfelter natural;
    endpapers—Multicolor Antique, thistle;
    cover (on .088 boards)—Holliston Roxite B (51588);
    and jacket—Permacote Offset, smooth finish,
        printed two colors (Black and PMS 199, Red),
        and varnished.

Production by Mercer Press Services.

Rust, Eric Charles.
The word and words : towards
a theology of preaching